Beagles as Pets

The Ultimate Beagle Owner's Guide

Beagle breeding, where to buy, types, care, temperament, cost, health, showing, grooming, diet, and much more included

By Lolly Brown

Copyrights and Trademarks

All rights reserved. No part of this book may be reproduced or transformed in any form or by any means, graphic, electronic, or mechanical, including photocopying, recording, taping, or by any information storage retrieval system, without the written permission of the author.

This publication is Copyright ©2016 NRB Publishing, an imprint. Nevada. All products, graphics, publications, software and services mentioned and recommended in this publication are protected by trademarks. In such instance, all trademarks & copyright belong to the respective owners. For information consult www.NRBpublishing.com

Disclaimer and Legal Notice

This product is not legal, medical, or accounting advice and should not be interpreted in that manner. You need to do your own due-diligence to determine if the content of this product is right for you. While every attempt has been made to verify the information shared in this publication, neither the author, neither publisher, nor the affiliates assume any responsibility for errors, omissions or contrary interpretation of the subject matter herein. Any perceived slights to any specific person(s) or organization(s) are purely unintentional.

We have no control over the nature, content and availability of the web sites listed in this book. The inclusion of any web site links does not necessarily imply a recommendation or endorse the views expressed within them. We take no responsibility for, and will not be liable for, the websites being temporarily unavailable or being removed from the internet.

The accuracy and completeness of information provided herein and opinions stated herein are not guaranteed or warranted to produce any particular results, and the advice and strategies, contained herein may not be suitable for every individual. Neither the author nor the publisher shall be liable for any loss incurred as a consequence of the use and application, directly or indirectly, of any information presented in this work. This publication is designed to provide information in regard to the subject matter covered.

Neither the author nor the publisher assume any responsibility for any errors or omissions, nor do they represent or warrant that the ideas, information, actions, plans, suggestions contained in this book is in all cases accurate. It is the reader's responsibility to find advice before putting anything written in this book into practice. The information in this book is not intended to serve as legal, medical, or accounting advice.

Foreword

Having a Beagle in your household is a journey towards getting to know one of the more unique dog breeds in the world. From their very colorful history, their soulful looks and loving nature, and a very stubborn and independent streak underlying their inner hound, you may sometimes wonder why it feels like you're dealing with two different dogs in one tiny body. Having a Beagle for a pet entails balancing the responsibilities of taking care of them and protecting them, versus respecting their independence while at the same time training their stubborn nature.

It's always a good idea to know as much as you can about your pets, and this is especially true for the seemingly harmless and self-effacing Beagle. If you've ever wondered why your tiny Beagle doesn't listen to you when you call, or why he doesn't seem to like being left alone, read on. Within these pages you'll find some insights into the nature of the little Beagle, with some tips for raising and caring for them, training them and grooming them, and how you can best take on the responsibility of being the owner of one very unique dog!

Table of Contents

Introduction 1
   Glossary of Dog Terms 2
Chapter One: Understanding Beagles 9
   Facts about Beagles 10
   Summary of Beagle Facts 13
   Beagle Breed History 15
   Types of Beagles 18
Chapter Two: Things to Know Before Getting a Beagle 21
   Do You Need a License? 22
   How Many Beagles Should You Keep? 23
   Do Beagles Get Along with Other Pets? 24
   How Much Does it Cost to Keep a Beagle? 25
      Initial Costs 25
   What are the Pros and Cons of Beagles? 27
      Pros for Beagles 27
      Cons for the Beagles 28
Chapter Three: Purchasing Your Beagle 29
   Where Can You Buy Beagles? 29
   Adopting from a Rescue 30
      United States Rescues: 30
      United Kingdom Rescues: 31

Australia Rescues 31

How to Choose a Reputable Beagle Breeder 32

Tips for Selecting a Healthy Beagle Puppy 33

Beagle-Proofing Your Home 34

Chapter Four: Caring for Your New Beagle 39

Habitat and Exercise Requirements for Beagles 40

Exercise Requirements for Beagles 41

Chapter Five: Meeting Your Beagle's Nutritional Needs 45

The Nutritional Needs of Dogs 46

Proteins 46

Carbohydrates 47

Fats 47

Vitamins and Minerals 47

How to Select a High-Quality Dog Food Brand 48

Understanding RER 49

Tips for Feeding Your Beagle 51

Dangerous Foods to Avoid 52

Chapter Six: Training Your Beagle 55

Socializing Your New Beagle Puppy 56

Crate Training - Housebreaking Your Puppy 58

Starting out your Beagle with a good Fetching Game 60

Positive Reinforcement and Rewards for Obedience 61

Chapter Seven: Grooming Your Beagle 63
Recommended Tools to Have on Hand 64
Tips for Bathing and Grooming Beagles 65
Other Grooming Tasks 66
Cleaning Your Beagle's Ears 66
Trimming Your Beagle's Nails 68
Brushing Your Beagle's Teeth 69

Chapter Eight: Breeding Your Beagle 71
Basic Dog Breeding Information 72
Breeding Tips and Raising Puppies 76

Chapter Nine: Showing Your Beagle 79
Beagle Breed Standard 80
Preparing Your Beagle for Show 81

Chapter Ten: Keeping Your Beagle Healthy 85
Common Health Problems Affecting Beagles 86
Epilepsy 86
Hypothyroidism 88
Chondrodystrophy or Dwarfism 89
Hip Dysplasia 91
Cherry Eye 92
Allergies 93
Obesity 94

  Musladin-Lueke Syndrome (MLS) 96
  Preventing Illness with Vaccinations 97
Beagle Care Sheet 101
  1.) Basic Beagle Information 101
  2.) Habitat Requirements 104
  3.) Nutritional Needs 104
  4.) Breeding Information 106
Index 109
Photo Credits 117
References 119

Introduction

One of the most popular dog breeds to keep as pets in the United States today is the Beagle. Quite apart from the breed's added popularity because of Peanut's Snoopy, dubbed "the most popular Beagle in the world," Beagles are just heartbreakingly adorable and cute. Compact in size without being too small, they are hardy and intelligent canines who are also friendly and sociable, with the irresistibly soft, pleading look of a hound.

One thing that Snoopy does reflect as a breed characteristic is an independent streak and stubborn nature. Beagles will make up their own minds about things, and

Introduction

their lives will not revolve around trying to please you. But that is indeed part of their charm. The key to understanding a Beagle is knowing what it is that drives them - which in most instances will be their nose.

Beagles are, in a word, scenthounds.

Glossary of Dog Terms

AKC – American Kennel Club, the largest purebred dog registry in the United States

Almond Eye – Referring to an elongated eye shape rather than a rounded shape

Babbler - A hound that gives tongue when not on the trail

Balance – A show term referring to all of the parts of the dog, both moving and standing, which produce a harmonious image

Bay - Prolonged bark of a hunting hound

Beard – Long, thick hair on the dog's underjaw

Best in Show – An award given to the only undefeated dog left standing at the end of judging

Bicolor - A coat of two distinct colors

Bitch – A female dog

Introduction

Bite – The position of the upper and lower teeth when the dog's jaws are closed; positions include level, undershot, scissors, or overshot

Blaze – A white stripe running down the center of the face between the eyes

Board – To house, feed, and care for a dog for a fee

Break - When the puppy's coat color changes as an adult

Breed – A domestic race of dogs having a common gene pool and characterized appearance/function

Breed Standard – A published document describing the look, movement, and behavior of the perfect specimen of a particular breed

Buff – An off-white to gold coloring

Castrate - The removal of the testicles of a male dog.

Character - The individuality, general appearance, expression and deportment considered typical of a breed.

Clip – A method of trimming the coat in some breeds

Coarse - Lacks refinement.

Coat – The hair covering of a dog; some breeds have two coats, and outer coat and undercoat; also known as a double coat. Examples of breeds with double coats include German Shepherd, Siberian Husky, Akita, etc.

Introduction

Condition – The health of the dog as shown by its skin, coat, behavior, and general appearance

Conformation - Form and structure of shape and parts in conformance with breed standards

Corky - Lively, active

Crate – A container used to house and transport dogs; also called a cage or kennel

Crossbreed (Hybrid) – A dog having a sire and dam of two different breeds; cannot be registered with the AKC

Cry - Baying or music of hounds

Dam (bitch) – The female parent of a dog;

Dock – To shorten the tail of a dog by surgically removing the end part of the tail.

Dominance - Displays of assertiveness of one dog over other dogs

Double Coat – Having an outer weather-resistant coat and a soft, waterproof coat for warmth; see above.

Drop Ear – An ear in which the tip of the ear folds over and hangs down; not prick or erect

Ear set - A description of where the ears are set on the head

Even bite - Also *level bite,* meeting of upper and lower incisors without any overlapping

Introduction

Ear leather - The flap of the ear

Feathering – A long fringe of hair on the ears, tail, legs, or body of a dog

Fetch - A game of retrieval

Gait - A pattern of steps with a particular rhythm and footfall

Game - Wild animals being hunted

Genealogy - Also *Pedigree*.

Gestation Period - From the time of mating until birth.

Gun dog - Dog trained to hunt game.

Groom – To brush, trim, comb or otherwise make a dog's coat neat in appearance

Heat - Estrus, fertile period of the female.

Heel – To command a dog to stay close by its owner's side

Hip Dysplasia – A condition characterized by the abnormal formation of the hip joint

Hound - Dogs that hunt game through scent or sight.

Hound-colored - Black, tan and white with a black saddle

Inbreeding – The breeding of two closely related dogs of one breed

Introduction

Interbreeding - The breeding of dogs of different breeds

Kennel – A building or enclosure where dogs are kept

Lead - Leash

Litter – A group of puppies born at one time

Markings – A contrasting color or pattern on a dog's coat

Mate – To breed a dog and a bitch

Milk teeth - Baby teeth

Mongrel - The result of crossbreeding

Neuter – To castrate a male dog or spay a female dog

Pack - Several hounds kept in one kennel

Pads – The tough, shock-absorbent skin on the bottom of a dog's foot

Parti-Color – A coloration of a dog's coat consisting of two or more definite, well-broken colors; one of the colors must be white

Pedigree – The written record of a dog's genealogy going back three generations or more

Point - A stylized stance of a hunting dog to indicate the location of game

Puppy – A dog under 12 months of age

Introduction

Purebred – A dog whose sire and dam belong to the same breed and who are of unmixed descent

Retrieve - Bringing back game to the hunter

Saddle - Dark patches over the back

Shedding – The natural process whereby old hair falls off the dog's body as it is replaced by new hair growth.

Sire – The male parent of a dog

Sighthound - Compare with general term Hound: Dogs that hunt by sight

Smooth Coat – Short hair that is close-lying

Spay – The surgery to remove a female dog's ovaries, rendering her incapable of breeding

Stud - Male dog used for breeding

Tricolor - a coat of three distinct colors, usually black, white and tan

Trim – To groom a dog's coat by plucking or clipping

Type - A sum of qualities distinguishing a specific breed or a specific dog

Undercoat – The soft, short coat typically concealed by a longer outer coat

Introduction

Wean – The process through which puppies transition from subsisting on their mother's milk to eating solid food

Whelping – The act of birthing a litter of puppies

Whiskers - Sensory organs consisting of hairs on the sides of a dog's muzzle

Chapter One: Understanding Beagles

Beagles are medium-sized hounds, generally described as miniature Foxhounds, with all of the same hound instincts deliberately bred into their tiny bodies over the years of their evolution.

Beagles are playful, cheerful, social, amiable and insatiably curious, and they make wonderful family pets. But perhaps the best showing of the Beagle's true nature is

Chapter One: Understanding Beagles

when he is out in the field, assisting a hunter in tracking and hunting game.

These days, the nearest activity to their original purpose that some Beagles are used for are as scent hounds tracking illegal or contraband agricultural imports in the border areas of the United States. This breed is popularly acknowledged to have one of the best scenting abilities among other dog breeds, recognizing nearly 50 distinct scents or odors.

Mostly, however, the modern Beagle lives the ordinary life of a contented household pet, living amidst their human family or pack, satisfying his hound instincts whenever he can. Prospective pet owners should be aware that those instincst will never be truly dormant in the indomitable Beagle.

If you're considering keeping a Beagle as a pet and wondering whether this is the right breed for you, read on for some interesting information about the unique traits, characteristics and history of this breed.

Facts about Beagles

While there is no accurate record of the origin of the name "Beagle," it is believed that the term may have been

Chapter One: Understanding Beagles

derived from the French word *begueule,* which means "open throat," or the Old English or Gaelic term *beag,* meaning "small." Another possible origin of the word is the German *begele,* meaning "to scold."

"Beagling," on the other hand, refers to the Beagle activity of hunting hares and rabbits, though not foxes, by scent. The Beagle packs are followed by the hunters, either on foot or mounted.

These meanings associated with the name of the Beagle should already alert you to one of the more peculiar characteristics of the tiny Beagle: that he is essentially a hunter, and has a healthy throat and vocal cords that they will certainly not hesitate to use.

The Beagle has three distinct vocalizations: the bark or the growl, a baying howl, and a half-baying howl (which sounds like a cross between frantic barking and a bay). This last, the half-howl, is what Beagles usually use to alert hunters to the fact that they have caught sight of their prey.

In fact, the white tip at the end of a Beagle's tail, also otherwise known as a "flag," is also a unique characteristic of the breed, and also designed to make him a more efficient hunting companion. Having been bred specifically to hunt rabbits, this tiny hound is easier to spot among the thick underbrush by the sight of their jaunty white tail sticking up above the tall grass.

Chapter One: Understanding Beagles

Beagles are also pack animals, which means that they do best in a group - and will not like to be left alone for long periods of time. Generally, they hunt better as a pack, though these days, and for the Beagle family pet, they prefer being in the company of their human family. If left alone for long periods of time, they will either grow anxious, or they will become bored. Either way, it can be a recipe for household chaos for this creative and very energetic breed. Sometimes you'll wonder how he ever managed to chew out of his wire cage, enter the pantry in the kitchen, and reach the food on one of the topmost shelves, all within the brief span of the thirty minutes that you were outside of the house!

Shall you yell at your Beagle? How could you? He looks so innocent, looking at you with those gentle, pleading eyes. Besides, he's so small and cute! Perhaps it was a freak accident, you say? No, of course not! Who else could it have been but him? He was the only one left in the house, after all.

Shall you yell at him now? Maybe not. I don't think he'll like that. Beagles don't like being yelled at. Besides, he was just following his nose. Why punish him for following one of his hardwired natural instincts? Besides, you should have known better than to leave your Beagle alone for long.

Chapter One: Understanding Beagles

One further interesting fact is that the AKC actually holds sanctioned field trials where a couple or packs of Beagles are put to the test out in the field tracking and scenting small game.

Summary of Beagle Facts

Pedigree: Talbot Hound, North Country Beagle, Southern Hound, and the Harrier

AKC Group: Hound Group

Types: In the AKC, distinction is made between two sizes - the 13-inch Beagle (no taller than 13 inches at the withers), and the 15-inch Beagle (between 13 and 15 inches at the withers). No size distinction is made in Kennel Groups of other countries.

Breed Size: small to medium size

Height: 13 to 16 inches (33 to 41 cm) high at the withers

Weight: 20 to 25 lb (9-11 kg)

Coat Length: medium length

Coat Texture: close and hard, hound coat

Color: Varied, may be tricolor or bi-color, usually of white, brown and black, with white as the predominant color, a

Chapter One: Understanding Beagles

black saddle, and tan or brown markings around the saddle. Bi-colors usually have white as the predominant color, with the secondary color as reddish, orange, liver, or blue (smoky gray).

Eyes and Nose: Dark brown or hazel eyes, black or gumdrop nose

Ears: Floppy or dropped ears, set slightly above the eyes and hanging close to the head

Tail: Set fairly high, short and slightly curved, with a white tip. It is held upright or carried in a jaunty fashion, and does not curve over the back.

Temperament: Friendly, has an even temper and gentle disposition; amiable. A bit excitable, easily distracted or bored.

Strangers: Beagles will bark or howl at anything or anyone unfamiliar, but they can be easily won over. They make good watchdogs but poor guard dogs.

Other Dogs: Beagles generally get along well with other dogs.

Other Pets: Generally friendly with other pets, and are actually quite gentle with cats.

Training: Difficult to train. Beagles are intelligent, but having been bred to be scenthounds, they are single-minded and focused when they pick up a scent. They are easily distracted by the smells around them. Obedience is not very high.

Exercise Needs: Regular moderate exercise such as daily walks, with occasional intense bursts of exercise such as running at least once a week.

Health Conditions: epilepsy, hypothyroidism, chondrodystrophy or dwarfism, hip dysplasia, cherry eye, allergies, obesity, Musladin-Lueke Syndrome (MLS)

Lifespan: average 12-15 years

Beagle Breed History

A closer look at the history of the Beagle breed will attest to the claim that breeding dogs is both a science and an art. The fact is, the modern Beagle is a pretty recent breed, and it did not develop in its present form until well into the 19th century.

Beagles as an scenthound breed, however, have been around for a long time - there have been references to such "small hounds that hunted by scent" as early as Ancient Greece, though there is no real way of proving that they were the Beagle's ancestors other than by surmise and deduction.

Chapter One: Understanding Beagles

The attempt at developing the "perfect hound" began sometime in the 11th century, when William the Conqueror brought the milk-white Talbot Hound - a now extinct species of hound - to Britain.

A series of crossbreeding then followed, as humans attempted to isolate the desirable traits in an idealized genetic mix. From the Greyhounds, it is said that they got their speed, and it is also surmised that earlier crossbreeding with Ireland's Kerry Beagle gave the Beagle its scenting ability.

The result was two breeds that came about sometime in the 18th century: the Southern Hound, and the Northern Hound. The Southern Hound - which is generally accepted to be the direct ancestor of the modern Beagle - was taller and heavier than the Northern breed. It was also slower, but it had better developed scenting abilities.

An interesting side-note here is that there were also known accounts of a "Pocket Beagle," and a "Glove Beagle," both of which are suspected to refer to one and the same breed. These were small hounds popular with the English Royalty, so named because they could fit into a pocket or a glove. There have been records of Queen Elizabeth I having a Pocket Beagle, and of Edward II and Henry VII with a Glove Beagle. As with the Talbot Hound, however, this tiny

Chapter One: Understanding Beagles

breed is also now extinct, thought to have been lost after Word War I.

Both larger and smaller hounds worked together during hunting activities, the smaller hounds pursuing the hunt through the thick underbrush after the larger hounds had run the prey to the ground.

Perhaps it was an attempt to combine the best of the larger and smaller breeds of hounds that led to further attempts at crossbreeding. The smaller Beagle types were crossed with larger breeds, and this resulted in the modern Foxhound. There were also smaller versions of this breed which nearly became extinct, were it not for their use as rabbit-hunting packs by some peasant farmers.

In the 1830s, one Reverend Phillip Honeywood set up his own Beagle pack in Essex, and many believe that his pack was the precursor of the modern Beagle. There are no detailed records of the crossbreeding undertaken with his pack, though it is believed that it included the Northern Beagle, the Southern Hound, and Harriers. The result was a small hound, about 10 inches at the shoulder, and were pure white. At this time, other Beagle packs were kept elsewhere, some by royalty such as Prince Albert and Lord Winterton, and other crossbreeding attempts in an effort to produce the ideal specimen that combined hunting ability and attractiveness.

In the years that followed, there were further differentiations in the results of crossbreeding, some with regards to size, others to hunting abilities, even in coat texture. The first standard description, however, was produced sometime in 1890, after the Beagle Club was formed in England.

The American Beagle standard, on the other hand, was believed to have stemmed from a bloodline imported from England and further developed by one General Richard Rowett in Illinois. They were accepted as a breed by the AKC only in 1884.

Types of Beagles

There are no differentiations in types of Beagles, though the AKC does recognize two different types based on size: the first is the 13-inch Beagle, standing less than 13 inches or 33 cm., and the 15-inch Beagle, or Beagles who are between 13 and 15 inches in height, or from 33 to 38 cm.

There are no such distinctions in other Kennel Clubs, as the UK Kennel Club recognizes a single type, with a height ranging from 13 to 16 inches (33 to 41 cm.), and the Canadian Kennel Club recognizes any height not exceeding 15 inches (38 cm.). Neither is any distinction recognized between American and English varieties, though it is

Chapter One: Understanding Beagles

commonly accepted that American Beagles are smaller by comparison.

It does not mean that Beagles whose height does not fall within those standards are not "Beagles" per se. Considering the breed's history of crossbreeding, the similarity in appearance with the Foxhound (which is of a significantly larger breed), and the innumerable variations of hounds produced by years of crossbreeding, the standard is perhaps just that - a standard. The standard height requirement is an ideal standard only, which apparently varies by country just as much as height can still vary among specific Beagles.

Though there is no longer a "Pocket Beagle," despite the claims of some modern breeders and owners. The bloodline of this strain became extinct long ago, and smaller than average Beagles nowadays are small only because they are either suffering from a genetic condition such as Dwarfism, severe malnourishment, or bad breeding.

It seems that these days, despite the modern Beagle's recognition as a distinct breed, crossbreeding attempts are still ongoing. The current trend nowadays is towards producing designer dogs, and one of the more popular crossbreeds is the "Puggle," or a cross between a Beagle and a Pug, apparently in an attempt to produce a Beagle that is at least less active and less excitable than its predecessor.

Chapter One: Understanding Beagles

Perhaps it is a misnomer to refer to a "purebred Beagle"?

In any case, the modern Beagle is a thriving breed, being popular family pets, and recognized by Kennel Clubs the world over. Despite the seeming inconvenience of the Beagle's unique traits and characteristics which discount them from being desired pets by certain living situations, they are still nurtured and appreciated today for the very qualities that brought them into being in the first place: their compact size, and their stubborn and unrelenting hunting instincts and scenthound abilities.

Chapter Two: Things to Know Before Getting a Beagle

Beagles are such cute and adorable pets that they can work their charms on pretty much everyone. But not everybody is cut out to be the owner of a Beagle. This breed has very unique quirks and specific qualities and characteristics that sometimes belie their seemingly angelic looks. If you are the type who likes quiet, calm and obedient pets, then perhaps the Beagle is not for you.

Assuming, however, that you are still determined to have a Beagle as a pet, following are some of the finer points about Beagle ownership to guide you.

Chapter Two: Things To Know Before Getting A Beagle

Do You Need a License?

Whether or not you are required to have a license for your pet depends on the laws and regulations of your specific region. The only real way to be certain is to do your research - consult with the local council of your area, and ask some of your neighbors who are also pet owners. An even better idea is to get hold of a copy of the local ordinance governing pet ownership and licenses in your area.

In general, however, most states do require owners to register and get a license for their dogs. This is usually coterminous with a proof of vaccination, and both expire at the same time. In a sense, proof of vaccination is a prerequisite for a license, and both need to be renewed annually. This shouldn't be a problem because responsible dog ownership requires you to get your dog his annual shots. Regardless of where you come down on the debate of annual booster shots (i.e., whether or not they are really necessary), rabies vaccinations are still a must.

Part of the benefit of having your dog registered and of getting a license is the ease of tracking ownership of your pet in case he gets lost, and this is especially true of your Beagle. In fact, it is recommended that regardless of whether or not your area expects you to get a license, Beagle owners should register and license their pets, and get the necessary identifying tags that he can wear around his

Chapter Two: Things To Know Before Getting A Beagle

collar. Some would even go so far as to have their Beagles microchipped.

This in itself should already warn you just how seriously you should take a Beagle's tendency to wander, and his dogged persistence in following whatever scent catches his attention. There is also the darker side of Beagle life - the reality that this breed, over other canine breeds, is the one most preferred for experimental testing. Be vigilant when it comes to your Beagle's safety, just as you would be with any member of your family.

How Many Beagles Should You Keep?

Beagles are pack animals, which means that they are certainly happier when in the company of other Beagles. The norm for the natural life of this breed is to move and hunt in packs - flushing out game from the underbrush, tracking them down, hunting them, and retrieving them for their human masters.

But not all Beagles live that life now. And while they will still prefer a large company, it doesn't mean that they will not be happy with a smaller pack - his human family.

Whether or not you will choose to keep more than one Beagle is up to you, of course. Just be aware that more Beagles means a higher cost of pet ownership, and more

Chapter Two: Things To Know Before Getting A Beagle

energy needed to exercise them, train them, and keep them happy.

Then again, keeping two Beagles, for instance, as a minimal number, might actually solve some of the dilemmas that come with Beagle ownership - keeping him from getting lonely and bored. If he has another Beagle (or another pet) to play with, then the less likely that he will want to chew through his cage or dig under the fence to get outside. Or will it? The niceties of pet ownership depend just as much on the prospective owner's preference as much as it does on each pet's individual traits and characteristics. Use your best judgment.

Do Beagles Get Along with Other Pets?

Beagles are notoriously friendly, and they will be amiable not only to his human family but his fellow pet bunkmates. You needn't have any undue worry on that score.

In fact, there are some who claim that Beagles are one of the best dog breeds to have in the house, alongside your cats, with whom they will show great tenderness and affection.

But this general friendliness should be taken with a grain of salt - especially when it comes to smaller animals

Chapter Two: Things To Know Before Getting A Beagle

like rabbits or hamsters. Don't underestimate the Beagle's hardwired hunting instincts, and don't forget that the Beagle's breeding history was specifically engineered to make them effective rabbit hunters out in the field.

Unless properly socialized when they were young, in fact, you should take this general warning as applicable to all other pets that are smaller than they are - including cats.

How Much Does it Cost to Keep a Beagle?

Initial Costs

The initial cost of a Beagle would depend on whether you acquire your new pet from a shelter, or whether you are purchasing a purebred with champion lineage. Adoption fees can range from $100 to $250, while purebred puppies can range from around $875 to $1,000.

Other initial costs to factor in include:

Spaying or Neutering	$200
Medical Examination	$70
Crate	$95
Training	$110
Leash and Collar	$30

Chapter Two: Things To Know Before Getting A Beagle

Total	$505

Add in the initial purchase price, registration or licensing fees, food and water bowls, dog toys, and various other supplies and accessories, and look to shelling out upwards of $1,000 on one-time costs for your first year, quite apart from the yearly costs such as food, vaccinations, medical checkups and grooming supplies.

An average breakdown of these yearly costs of owning one Beagle can be seen in the table below:

	In USD	based on conversion rate of 1GBP=1.438 USD	based on conversion rate of 1USD=1.303 AUD
Food expenses	$525	£365.21	684.07 AUD
Veterinarian Bills	$699	£486.25	910.79 AUD
Other costs (toys, treats and other accessories)	$545	£379.12	710.13 AUD

Chapter Two: Things To Know Before Getting A Beagle

Total	$1,769	£1,230.58	2,304.99 AUD

The above projected costs are only an estimate, and do not factor in the cost of Beagle-proofing your home, including the installation of a secure fence in your yard, or the wear and tear or possible destruction of household objects or furniture. Nor does it factor in medical expenses should your Beagle prove to have an ailment or medical condition.

Overall, Beagles are not very expensive to keep. They fall somewhere within the middle range of pet costs and expenses when compared with other breeds.

What are the Pros and Cons of Beagles?

Pros for Beagles

- Easy to groom and care for

- Gets along well with children and other pets, making them good family pets
- Lovable and amiable
- Not picky eaters
- Good retrievers and will love to play
- Intelligent once properly trained
- Overall health is good
- Make good watchdogs
- Small and low maintenance pets

Cons for the Beagles

- Being pack animals, Beagles are prone to separation anxiety
- Easily bored and distracted
- Stubborn and a bit difficult to train
- Loves to eat, so has a tendency to become overweight
- Can be loud pets to keep
- Requires constant supervision
- Housetraining can be challenging

Chapter Three: Purchasing Your Beagle

So you've done your homework on the nature, characteristics, and quirks of the Beagle. If the thought of having one for a pet still appeals to you, it is time to look into the particulars of where to get one. This chapter also gives you tips on how to select a healthy puppy from a litter, and how to puppy-proof your home.

Where Can You Buy Beagles?

Unless you personally know someone who has a Beagle mother that's about to have a litter of puppies, you have two options: you can either buy one from a breeder, or you can adopt one.

Adopting from a Rescue

Adopting a Beagle from a rescue should always be considered first before you consider purchasing a newborn puppy. There are many Beagles, and other dog breeds, in need of rescue and with no home to go to. Following are lists of Beagle rescues in the United States, the UK, and Australia, which you can explore or use as the starting point for your search. A simple online search will easily lead you to one closer to your place of residence.

United States Rescues:

Hound Rescue in the Central Texas Area http://www.houndrescue.com/

SOS Beagle Rescue, Inc. http://www.sosbeagles.org/

A list of Beagle Rescues from adoptapet.com http://www.adoptapet.com/s/adopt-a-beagle

Brew Inc. http://www.brewbeagles.org/

A list of Beagle Rescues from onegreenplanet.org
http://www.onegreenplanet.org/animalsandnature/10-awesome-beagle-rescue-groups-in-the-u-s/

Beagle Freedom Project
http://www.beaglefreedomproject.org/

United Kingdom Rescues:

Beagle Welfare http://www.beaglewelfare.org.uk/

dogsblog.com http://www.dogsblog.com/category/beagle/

Beagle Dogs and Puppies for Adoption in the UK http://www.pets4homes.co.uk/adoption/dogs/beagle/

A listing of Beagle Rescues from The Kennel Club http://www.thekennelclub.org.uk/services/public/findarescue/Default.aspx?breed=1005

East Cascade Beagle Rescue
http://www.cascaderescue.org/labdivision_faq.html

Australia Rescues

Beagle Rescue of Queensland
http://www.beagleclubqld.org/after-a-beagle/beagle-rescue

Chapter Three: Purchasing Your Beagle

Beagle Rescue & Rehoming
http://www.beaglerescuensw.org.au/

Beagle Freedom Australia http://beaglefreedomaustralia.org/

Beagle Rescue Victoria
https://www.petrescue.com.au/groups/10359

How to Choose a Reputable Beagle Breeder

If you would rather have a newborn Beagle puppy, then your search should start with figuring out who are the reputable breeders in your area. Try starting with an inquiry with your local Kennel Club - they usually have a current list of whom they consider reputable breeders in your area.

This is a time to be cautious and discerning. There are many amateur breeders out there who are only in it for the money, and who will sell you puppies without any warranty for their medical or physical condition. They may claim to be reputable and that their breeding stock is strong, but how can you really tell?

First, ask around. If it is a reputable breeder, then he or she will already have an established reputation in your area. And what could be better than a testament from those who have already purchased Beagles from them before?

Chapter Three: Purchasing Your Beagle

When you meet them, be prepared to ask questions about the breed, about the breeding process, and about the parents of this particular litter. You might even request a view of the facilities and the litter itself. Is the area clean and do the dogs look happy, well fed and clean? Feel free to satisfy your curiosity. If it is a reputable breeder, they should be just as willing and happy to answer all your questions and provide you with all the information you need.

You should also ask about the process for purchasing a puppy. Generally, a deposit is required, which would also serve as your reservation. A reputable breeder usually has a list of ready and willing potential owners just waiting for the puppies to be weaned, so you should be ready to act quickly once your decision has been made and all your questions satisfied.

Tips for Selecting a Healthy Beagle Puppy

Aside from picking out the one puppy who most appeals to you, there really isn't much to be said for picking out your puppy from the litter. Pick one who seems healthy and active, though not too wild - the one that is clean and with a good physique and who is friendly rather than shy.

Chapter Three: Purchasing Your Beagle

That is why it is extremely important to choose a reputable breeder to begin with. If you've done your homework on the person who bred the puppies, the history of the Beagle parents and the type and quality of offspring they produce, then you should rest assured that whichever puppy you pick will likely be a healthy and well-adjusted one, with minimal chances of having or being carriers of genetic defects or other health conditions.

If you have satisfied yourself on these points, then you can simply go with which puppy you feel you have the most connection with, the one that seems to have the makings of your lifelong companion. Regardless of size or color or whether it seems to be the most dominant pup or not, as long as you have been thorough with your background check and preselection research, you are at least assured that it will be a healthy and fit puppy.

Beagle-Proofing Your Home

Beagle-proofing your home is certainly a project unto itself. Dog-proofing is not the same as Beagle-proofing. To truly Beagle-proof your home, you have to be doubly conscientious, even creative in your outlook. Even then, your pet Beagle may still surprise you. It's probably

Chapter Three: Purchasing Your Beagle

accurate to say that Beagle-proofing your home will prove to be a lifelong task.

You will have two things working against you: the Beagle's natural curiosity, and the fact that Beagles are easily bored. It's part of their cute, lovable little package to get into scrapes you never even imagined possible, while looking completely like an innocent angel at the same time.

Should you leave them alone for any length of time, they will paw around, poke around, smell around, and chew around. Add the fact that they will likely dig around if you leave them in the yard instead.

The most effective obedience training will only go so far in limiting their kind of scrapes they will get into, and it will never truly breed out of them their natural curiosity and attraction to particular scents or smells. The most that you can do is make sure that they are safe even as they explore the world around them, by removing from their reach anything that will prove dangerous or toxic to them.

Look around your home and try to eliminate or at least minimize the following:

- Loose wires, cords, or low-hanging curtains and table cloths or clothes. They will pull at them and they will chew their way through. Keep these safely secured and out of your Beagle's reach, especially the electrical wires and cords to keep them from accidental electrocution or strangling.

- Poisonous or toxic plants in your yard or in your house. The danger of poisonous substances also applies to medicines, household cleaners and any chemicals you may have left lying around. And close the lid of the toilet bowl, too.
- Secure open sources of water like swimming pools or drums of water. Beagles are not good swimmers. You might also want to secure open sources of fire like fireplaces and grills.
- Store and put away food items, and secure the lid of your trash cans. Aside from the chaos of them getting into your pantry or the trash and making a complete mess, they might ingest something which is not good for them. Remember that not all "people food" are safe for dogs to eat, and remember also that Beagles love to eat - they will most likely follow their nose to things that smell edible and good. Never underestimate a Beagle's nose, and his stubbornness at following wherever it leads him.
- Don't leave any of your important documents lying around. Aside from a tendency to chew things, they will also shred things. On that note, you might want to make sure that they will not be able to get at any of your shoes or into your closet, too.

Chapter Three: Purchasing Your Beagle

- Secure the yard - preferably with a locked and dug-in fence that will be truly effective in keeping a Beagle confined. Make doubly sure of this. If there is any weak link in your fence, like a gap large enough for him to fit through, or a weak link in the soil or in the fence that he can dig his way under, you can be certain that he will find it. For his own safety, test each area of the fence around your yard.

There are probably a lot more possibilities for mischief that a Beagle can see around your house aside from those mentioned above. Before bringing your new pet home, try going around, imagining how things would look to a very curious and bored animal. You might even want to get down on all fours to see things from his literal perspective. You'll probably find a lot more things that would need to be secured or stored elsewhere. Just remember that to a Beagle, everything is fair game - particularly when he still hasn't been trained.

No matter how conscientious you may be in Beagle-proofing your home, however, it is almost always a certainty that he will do something completely unexpected which you never even imagined - creating a big mess in the process. A big part of their intelligence is, after all, a natural curiosity about the world and the will and resolve to satisfy that curiosity.

Chapter Three: Purchasing Your Beagle

Remember that this is only natural to them, and try not to get mad. Beagles simply do not respond well to anger or punishment. Just be clear in your signals and cues as you continue training them to obey your various commands.

Having a Beagle for a pet can be a frustrating experience, but it can also be extremely rewarding. Be firm, give them a healthy diet and plenty of regular exercise, and above all, be patient with them. Sooner or later, they might actually surprise you with unexpected moments of good behavior!

Chapter Four: Caring for Your New Beagle

So now that you've brought your Beagle home, you're probably wondering what's the best way to take care of him and how to keep him healthy and happy. Read on for some Beagle-specific guidelines and tips on taking care of your new pet.

Chapter Four: Caring for Your New Beagle

Habitat and Exercise Requirements for Beagles

Here are a few facts about the Beagle breed that may guide you as you set them up in their new home:

- They are pack animals, which means that they do not like being left alone for long or they might become bored and try to escape, or become destructive.
- Beagles are a very active and high energy breed, so having a fenced-in yard for them to play in is highly recommended
- Beagles can be quite noisy.

Fact is, Beagles have three recognized types of calls: the bark, the bay, and the howl. To them, it's second nature, and part of their genetic makeup as hounds. But if you are type of person who prefers quiet dogs, then the Beagle is probably not for you. On the other hand, if you live in an area where neighbors live close and will not appreciate nightly howls, then you might want to think twice about whether a Beagle is the perfect pet for your home.

That aside, Beagles are highly adaptable pets, and they are generally friendly to kids, people, and other animals. They will get along well with most people, in fact, even strangers, so it isn't a good idea to use them as guard

Chapter Four: Caring for Your New Beagle

dogs. They do make great family pets. Provide them with a quality dog bed in one corner of your house - away from the constant barrage of noise and lights, so that he can get some quality sleep, too. Try not to start him on the habit of sleeping on your bed - you'll probably regret it when the seasons turn and it comes time for him to shed.

It is up to you as the owner whether you'd rather leave him outside in the yard at night, or whether you'll keep him inside. But be aware that aside from Beagles being wanderers, with a tendency for digging and for following their nose whenever the fancy takes them, there is also a distinct possibility that they might be stolen if you do leave them outside. Beagles are generally friendly with strangers, and they are one of the breeds most used for experimental testing, mainly because of their docile nature. Whichever you decide, try to keep their safety uppermost in your mind.

Exercise Requirements for Beagles

Having been bred to be scenthounds, Beagles were not meant to be cooped up inside the house. Provide them with their daily walk - this would give them a chance to exercise their legs and explore the neighborhood, allowing them to utilize their sense of smell and to also provide them with mental stimulation. Always have your Beagle on a

Chapter Four: Caring for Your New Beagle

leash when you do go out - Beagles are wanderers, and they have a tendency to be tenacious when they have picked up a scent which appeals to them.

In addition to their daily walks, additional play is also recommended, since Beagles have a lot of energy to spare. A good fetching game can test their agility, their capacity to obey commands such as "fetch" and "come," and it will also engage their natural retriever instincts. An alternative would be - if you have the good fortune to live in the countryside where hunting for wild game is permitted - the scenting, tracking, and hunting for wild rabbits.

If you and your Beagle are city dwellers, however, there are other alternatives you may try. You can set up a scenting or hunting game for them, where they will be retrieving hidden objects for you. You might be surprised at how fast and effective scenthounds they can be. But you shouldn't be, really - it is a nature of the breed, which general fact must already be known to you.

If you do have the time and the opportunity for it, you can make these little mental games more creative and challenging for your Beagle. If you don't want to do that, then you can probably mix it up with running or jogging as an alternative - but always in addition to their regular walks.

How much exercise of each should you give them? For an average adult of good health, a daily walk once a day,

Chapter Four: Caring for Your New Beagle

and more intense activities such as running or other games at least once a week, should be sufficient. You would necessarily need to make adjustments for various conditions such as when your pet is sick, when he is becoming overweight, or for varying weather conditions.

It is always a good idea to have your Beagle go for a complete physical examination before you undertake putting him on any exercise regimen. You would need to satisfy yourself that your Beagle is completely healthy and capable of meeting the demands of daily exercise. But it is also an opportune time to have a discusion with your veterinarian regarding his recommendations or opinions on your pet's proposed exercise regimen. Be watchful of the results - if your pet is easily tired, perhaps you are giving him more exercise than he can handle. But if he is still pretty hyper at the end of the day, perhaps you haven't been giving him enough. Adjust accordingly.

Start them out when they are young. Beagles tend to grow lazy as they mature, and once they have gotten used to long naps and start becoming obese, it might become challenging to have them go for their regular walks. Regular exercise will ward off the weight gain to which this heavy-eating breed is prone to. If they do not get their regular exercise, they will certainly become bored, and this can lead to all sorts of destructive behavior.

Chapter Four: Caring for Your New Beagle

Chapter Five: Meeting Your Beagle's Nutritional Needs

Beagles as a breed are not picky about food - which is a mild way of saying that they'll pretty much eat anything you give them. And then some! With the growing rate of obesity in dogs, and with Beagles in particular, it is the responsibility of the owner to set the restrictions and limitations - because your Beagle certainly will not!

Have a set schedule for feeding, twice a day for an ordinary, healthy Beagle. Some owners would even limit this to one feeding per day, especially if the Beagle's lifestyle allows for lots of snacks and treats throughout the day. But

Chapter Five Meeting Your Beagle's Nutritional Needs

what is the best dog food for a Beagle, and how much should you give them? Read on for some general guidelines on the nutritional needs of dogs, including some tips on feeding Beagles.

The Nutritional Needs of Dogs

Always remember to make drinking water readily available to your Beagle. This is a very active breed, and he will lose a lot of water in his daily activities, which he will need to replenish to keep from being dehydrated. Don't wait until you see him growing thirsty before offering him water to drink. Make water freely available to him to keep him from suffering from any of the symptoms of dehydration on the first place.

As for the food, there are some basic nutritional needs that all dogs need in their daily diet. Below is a short list of these nutritional requirements and a short description of each.

Proteins

Mainly obtained from meat and most meat-based products, protein is essential for growth and cell

Chapter Five Meeting Your Beagle's Nutritional Needs

regeneration and repair, and for Beagles especially, are necessary to help maintain their coat or fur. Be aware that experts do not recommend feeding your dog raw eggs, as this may have actually be harmful to their health.

Carbohydrates

This is usually derived from fiber-based products, and help in maintaining the intestinal health of your pet. Some carbohydrates can even be a good source of energy for your pet.

Fats

Fats provide your pet with a concentrated source of energy, and are also essential for some vitamins (A, E, D and K) to be absorbed. They help in protecting the internal organs and are vital in cellular production.

Vitamins and Minerals

Vitamins and minerals usually cannot be synthesized by a dog's body, so the primary source of these are the

Chapter Five Meeting Your Beagle's Nutritional Needs

synthesized versions obtainable in commercially available quality dog foods. Vitamins and minerals help in the normal functioning of their bodies, and also helps maintain their bones and teeth.

Thankfully, these daily nutritional needs are already given components in many of the commercially available dog food these days. So the next question is, how do you select a high quality dog food brand?

How to Select a High-Quality Dog Food Brand

Dogs are omnivores, which means that they will eat both meat and vegetables. That said, most experts recommend selecting a dog food brand that is meat-based instead of vegetable-based because your pet dog will likely not get much meat-based nutrients in his diet outside of what he gets from dog food. It isn't advisable to start feeding him meat directly, either. Loose bits of bone can get caught in his throat, causing a lot of trouble for the tiny breed, aside from the fact that it is inadvisable to have him start expecting that he will be eating meat regularly.

The next best thing, therefore, is a high quality meat-based dog food. Read the label. You can usually tell from

Chapter Five Meeting Your Beagle's Nutritional Needs

the first two or three ingredients which are meat-based and which are vegetable-based. Opt for dry instead of canned dog food as much as possible, and limit the treats you give them outside of their regular feeding schedule, especially if you give them as rewards during training. Those calories can pile up a lot more quickly than you think.

Understanding RER

The next question you will probably ask is how much? How much dog food do you give your Beagle at each feeding?

It's probably best to consult with your veterinarian at the beginning, to establish the recommended feeding portion for your Beagle. Because the truth is that there is no standard answer for all dogs, even if they are of the same breed.

You'll probably also come across the term RER during the course of your research, and might be wondering what this is. Basically, RER stands for Resting Energy Requirement, and is used as the basis for determining each dog's daily energy needs. The theory is that each dog's daily energy needs will be based on his weight, determined

Chapter Five Meeting Your Beagle's Nutritional Needs

according to a standard formula. For dogs weighing between 2 and 45 kg (5-99 lbs.), the formula for RER is:

RER = 30 (body weight in kilograms) + 70

It doesn't stop there. The result is the daily energy requirement of your Beagle while he is at rest. When he stops being at rest, that number changes. Below is a table containing some of these canine life changes and the recommended diet adjustment for each:

Neutered Adult	RER x 1
Intact Adult	RER x 1.6
Moderate Work Adult	RER x 3
Pregnant dog in the last 21 days before birth	RER x 3
Weaning Puppy	RER x 3
Adolescent Puppy	RER x 2
Obese Puppy undergoing weight loss activities	RER x 1

But these are only standard recommendations, and must always be adjusted to your Beagle's specific needs. Again, it is advisable that you ask your veterinarian the next

Chapter Five Meeting Your Beagle's Nutritional Needs

time you bring your Beagle for a checkup, just to establish what is a good amount to give your Beagle at each feeding.

Once you've done this, the next thing you should do is to pay attention. Does your Beagle seem energetic and healthy, or lethargic and lacking in interest and appetite? Does he look like he's growing a bit bulky around the waist? Has he not had much exercise the past few days because of bad weather conditions? Adjust the food you give him each time, decreasing or increasing according to your best judgment. But only if this means small or incremental changes. Don't make any major or drastic dietary changes unless you have first consulted with a professional.

Tips for Feeding Your Beagle

Beagles love food, so feeding them should not be too complicated. But armed with this knowledge, you can probably work their love of food elsewhere into their daily lifestyle, too.

Aside from the usual food-as-reward incentive during training, you can try and test their hound skills by having them scent out and track their food. You may be surprised at just how "dogged" and persistent they could be. But you shouldn't, really. They are one of the best scenting and tracking hounds there is. What better way then, to exercise them and nurture their natural talents by using one of the best Beagle motivators of all - food!

Create a lengthy tracking path using some of his most favorite treats. Or make it challenging by hiding the food somewhere in a large yard or a challenging terrain. Be creative - though always keep in mind their tendency to wander and be distracted by various scents. By making a game of it, you nurture their natural instinct and skills, their love of play and food, and give them physical exercise and mental stimulation at the same time!

Dangerous Foods to Avoid

In the same way that Beagles will not care how much they eat or how often, they will also not likely care what they eat. This can oftentimes be dangerous, especially when they come into contact with certain "people-food" that are actually dangerous for dogs to ingest.

Below is a list of some of these foods that you should never feed your Beagle. If they did ingest or swallow any of the following, you should bring them immediately to the nearest veterinarian.

Chapter Five Meeting Your Beagle's Nutritional Needs

- Alcohol
- Apple seeds
- Avocado
- Cherry pits
- Chocolate
- Citrus
- Coconut
- Coffee
- Garlic
- Grapes/raisins
- Hops
- Macadamia nuts
- Milk and Dairy
- Mold
- Mushrooms
- Mustard seeds
- Onions/leeks
- Peach pits
- Potato leaves/stems
- Raw meat and eggs
- Rhubarb leaves
- Salty snacks
- Tea
- Tomato leaves/stems
- Walnuts
- Xylitol
- Yeast dough

Chapter Five Meeting Your Beagle's Nutritional Needs

Chapter Six: Training Your Beagle

Let it be said here and now that training Beagles is...difficult.

Beagles are intelligent, loving and amiable creatures, but they are also fiercely independent, with a strong stubborn streak. It goes with the genes - they have been specifically bred to be hounds, with a very powerful sense of smell, and the determination to follow it wherever it leads them. Once they are on the trail of a particular scent, it may be difficult for you to even get them to notice you. One of the best things you can do, therefore, when you first undertake to train your Beagle, is to adjust your expectations.

Training a Beagle is not impossible, but be aware that it will require a lot of time and effort on your part. And lots of patience.

You might want to begin training your Beagle from the first moment you bring your puppy home. Start them when they're young, and they would not develop many of the undesirable habits which would be hard to break once they're older. For an older Beagle, a lot more patience is needed, but training is still a worthwhile undertaking.

Socializing Your New Beagle Puppy

Beagles are a social breed, though of course they would still need time to adjust to being a member of the human world. Socialization should start early, which shouldn't be very difficult because Beagles are naturally friendly with most everyone - strangers and other pets included. They respond well to praises and treats, which is also key to their further training. Getting angry with them or violence of any sort will just produce a maladjusted puppy, unless they learn to tune you out completely.

Chapter Six: Training Your Beagle

Socialization continues outside the home when you begin taking the Beagle out for its daily walk. A reliable leash is absolutely necessary. Their hound instincts are hardwired into them, and when caught by a particular curious scent, they will follow it. They will also wander on their own, which means a higher likelihood that they will get lost, or that you will lose them. Even if on a leash, you might find it difficult to get them to listen to you once they are on a hound trail.

Obedience training will take place in time. For now, the purpose is to get them to explore the world and to socialize them, exposing them to new sights and sounds, and the presence of other humans and possibly other animals. Be aware also that Beagles can be pretty yappy. They will bark and bay and howl - which means you probably shouldn't bring them anywhere where loud noises are not appreciated. It has been suggested that their name "Beagle" actually comes from the French word "begueule" which means "open throat," or "beugler" which means "to bellow." It's part of the hound package - to follow a scent trail and then to lead you to what he has found. This should probably already tell you that small apartments with close neighbors is not an ideal place to keep a Beagle.

It is recommended that you allow them a fenced-in yard to play in. This is a high-energy breed, with natural instincts that need to be satisfied outside of the usual daily

Chapter Six: Training Your Beagle

walks. Some play is to be expected, and since he is a naturally friendly breed, playing with the kids or other pets can further help him with his socialization skills.

Though again, be aware of the Beagle's tendency to wander. Also be aware that Beagles are friendly even to strangers, and they are one of the most stolen breeds on account of their popularity as animal test subjects. We need not go into that controversy right now, but suffice it to say that you need to be constantly watchful of your Beagle.

Don't leave them alone for long periods of time. They are pack animals, and they need company. And when they are allowed out of the house, keep them under constant watch and supervision, for their own safety.

Crate Training - Housebreaking Your Puppy

There are some who claim that it can take you up to a full year to fully housebreak your Beagle puppy. Done in the right way, however, it need not take that long. The most popular recommendation for housebreaking Beagle puppies is the use of Crate Training.

Crate Training works on the principle that dogs will not soil the place where they sleep. You will have to provide him with a closed cage that is large enough for him to move

Chapter Six: Training Your Beagle

around in. Also provide him with a blanket and a toy to keep him occupied while he is there. You will have to keep him confined within this space for certain periods of time - especially if you are out of the house and the puppy is left alone. This period of confinement will be interrupted by occasional periods of freedom when you take him out into the yard so he can do his business. The key is a regular feeding and yard schedule, and clear signals or cues from you on what is expected of him.

If you find him doing his business inside the crate, a clear and solid "No," and a note of disapproval will make it clear to him that the behavior is not desired. Conversely, clear praise and reward when he does what is desired - doing it out in the yard - will let him know what you expect of him.

Done repetitive and consecutively, the Beagle himself will start to feel that it is not a normal thing to do his business inside the crate or anywhere inside the house. Like a habit that needs to be coaxed steadily and slowly, he will pick it up soon enough - just trust in his intelligence. Meanwhile, be consistent, be patient, and don't let yourself be carried away by your own frustration.

Chapter Six: Training Your Beagle

Starting out your Beagle with a good Fetching Game

Hand in hand with housebreaking your Beagle puppy, one of the first things you can do to begin training them is to teach them how to fetch.

Much of the Beagle's instincts revolve around the hunt, so a game of retrieval will engage his natural instincts, allow him a time of playful romping around, and begin his training with a command that will at least be enjoyable to him. Once he gets the hang of it, and you demonstrate your approval and praise, the teaching and learning expereince will be a lot more enjoyable for both of you, which will also make him more open to learning other things.

Start out at a close distance to each other, indicating the object on the ground and have him bring it to you, clearly enunciating the word "Fetch." Using the word "Come" will also teach him to return to you whenever he hears the same word. Once he does this, reward him with words of praise or a treat. You can then try to increase the distance from where you are standing and where you toss the object. Occasionally, you may vary the object he has to retrieve, even the place where you conduct your training lessons. The core of what you are teaching will create its own impression on the Beagle puppy.

Chapter Six: Training Your Beagle

Do this for at least 20 minutes every day at first. Occasionally, once the command has been learned, you can do it once or twice each week, as you also begin to explore other Beagle training lessons and games.

Following on the idea of engaging a Beagle's hound instincts, you might want to look into home tracking or scenting activities that engage his superior sense of smell.

Positive Reinforcement and Rewards for Obedience

Beagles do not respond well to harsh or negativee treatment. Therefore, you must find a way to encourage him using reinforcement such as praise, and the occasional food treats or rewards.

Using food treats should be fairly easy. Beagles love to eat, and they will do a lot of things for food. They may not do it to please you, but they will do it if you feed them something tasteful. But a word of caution here: the increasing incidence of Beagle obesity can mostly be traced back to unscheduled and excessive treats being fed to these cute and lovable pets. You don't want him growing fat almost immediately even while he is still a puppy, and you certainly don't want him paying attention to you simply because you are offering him food as a bribe.

Chapter Six: Training Your Beagle

So while it is good idea to use food rewards as an incentive to training, use it sparingly. Praise or belly rubs can work just as well, and these might even strengthen the bond between you, while teaching him not to expect to be fed each time he does what you tell him to.

A further word about food rewards: Beagles take their food seriously. Don't tease them with it, waving a cookie in front of him before withdrawing it, or using it to lead him on, frustrating him at every turn. It will definitely not create a positive experience for your Beagle, and he will probably only learn to be wary and distrustful whenever it is feeding time. So respect the Beagle, and respect his love for food, in much the same way that you would do the same for humans.

Chapter Seven: Grooming Your Beagle

Grooming time is one of the best times to strengthen the bond between owner and Beagle. Grooming includes bathing, brushing their coats, cleaning their ears, trimming their nails and brushing their teeth.

Grooming Beagles is not necessarily a complicated thing. Their coat hairs are short, or medium-length, so while some regularity is called for, each session need not be as complicated and need not take as long as it would for longer-haired breeds. And if you get them used to regular grooming early on, ideally as soon as you bring them home

Chapter Seven: Grooming Your Beagle

as puppies, they would have gotten used to, maybe even liked, these grooming sessions so they shouldn't be quite as difficult or stubborn, particularly when it comes to cleaning their sensitive ears.

And yes, Beagles need regular grooming. Being built closer to the ground than other dogs, and whose regular activities include running or sniffing along the ground, they may pick up parasites or fleas, and grass seeds may even become trapped in their eyes or ears.

Also be aware that Beagles shed, so regular brushing is recommended. Their natural curiosity may also lead them to pick up dirt or mud, and every so often, you may notice them starting to get smelly. A bath would then be in order. Read on for some further tips on grooming your beloved Beagle.

Recommended Tools to Have on Hand

- bristle brush
- grooming mitt or de-shedding tool such as a hound glove with raised rubber nodes
- doggy bath products
- dog nail clippers
- dog ear cleaners

Chapter Seven: Grooming Your Beagle

- dog toothpaste and toothbrush
- canine eye wipes

Tips for Bathing and Grooming Beagles

Beagles have a smooth, dense double coat that is resistant to rain and a lot of dirt or debris. Hence they may look clean enough, but brushing is recommended at least once a week, or once every three days. Shed hair may have been caught up in the thick coat, and you'll surprise yourself at just how much excess hair you will manage to remove when you brush. Doing so will also stimulate the natural oils that keep their coats clean and shiny, and will also help to catch and remove various invisible pests and fleas that may have taken up residence in your Beagle's coat without either of you knowing where or when he picked them up. Not to mention that regular brushing will keep him looking clean and healthy.

Baths can be given at least once a month, or more if your Beagle seems to warrant it. Because of their small size, you can start giving your Beagle puppy a bath right at the sink, which they will fit more easily than a bathtub. Use quality dog shampoo, and be careful around the eyes. You may want to use some canine eye wipes to clean away the discharges that may have gathered in the corners of their eyes. Rinse thoroughly in order to remove soap residue from the coat, which might otherwise cause itchiness.

Be gentle, thorough, and try to create a positive experience for your pet throughout the entire process. This is an opportune time for you as the owner to thoroughly get to know your pet. Become familiar with their physical condition, run your hands along their coats, underbellies, neck and throat. Done regularly, this would enable you to catch any physical anomalies as quickly as possible. Regular grooming and bathing thus becomes another way for you to safeguard your Beagle's health.

Other Grooming Tasks

Cleaning Your Beagle's Ears

One of the reasons that a Beagle is such an effective scent hound is because of the peculiar shape and position of their ears. Hanging close to the ground when they are sniffing a trail, it helps trap the scent they are following close to their nose, enabling them to better isolate it from all other scents.

But also because of its peculiar shape and position, it can be the perfect breeding ground for bacterial infections.

Chapter Seven: Grooming Your Beagle

Air does not always circulate correctly inside the ears, and water or moisture can actually be trapped inside them. More than with any other breed, cleaning a Beagle's ears should be made a necessary part of their regular grooming ritual.

Use professionally-recommended quality ear cleaner. With a few drops into the ear, and a gentle massage at the base, wax buildup should be loosened, which you can then wipe off with clean gauze, unless he shakes them loose first by shaking his head.

Be gentle and patient, especially at first. Remember that Beagles' ears are sensitive, so it is very possible that you might cause him some injury if you are reckless. If you are unsure of what to do, have a professional show you how it's done. And try to create a positive experience for your pet around the experience, so that she does not become fearful or stressed out, which would only have her moving around restlessly or anxiously, which is certainly not advisable during such a sensitive procedure.

Once she realizes that there's nothing to fear, she'll sit quietly enough for you until you're done. Again, it's best to start them out early. Ear cleaning is recommended at least once every month, or more if warranted by excessive wax buildup. Be watchful, and pay attention if you notice her beginning to scratch at her ears, shaking her head, or if you

Chapter Seven: Grooming Your Beagle

notice a bad smell. The Beagle's ears should also be kept dry or bacteria might build up in trapped water or moisture.

Trimming Your Beagle's Nails

Trimming a Beagle's nails can be done once every five or six weeks, or when you start hearing his nails clacking on the hardwood floor. You don't want them growing too long or they might get caught on and tear on something, injuring your pet. Regularly trimming their nails also keeps them presentable and neat.

You will need regular dog nail clippers or a nail grinder. Be careful when you cut or grind - the quick, or the vessel that supplies blood to the nails - may be close to the nail's edge. If you do cut this, there will be bleeding, which you can treat immediately with some styptic powder or even lip balm.

Ask a professional to show you how it's done at first until you get the hang of it. Again, try to make it a positive experience for your pet so that he eventually realizes that there's nothing to worry about. Once they understand this, they will sit still long enough, making the process much faster to finish.

Chapter Seven: Grooming Your Beagle

Brushing Your Beagle's Teeth

Brush your Beagle's teeth once a day, or at least once every other day. Use quality dog toothbrush and toothpaste, lifting the outer lips to facilitate the process.

Again, this is a grooming task that you can start with the Beagle when they are still puppies. Be gentle, and you may want to start out by using a finger instead of a toothbrush, just getting them used to the feeling of it. If you don't reach the entire set of teeth at the first try, be satisfied with what you can reach. Just be patient. Once they have gotten used to it - and to sitting still with their teeth bared - you'll eventually be able to reach their full set of teeth.

Chapter Seven: Grooming Your Beagle

Chapter Eight: Breeding Your Beagle

Being such a significant step that is fraught with so much responsibility, the question of whether or not to breed your Beagle must always be accompanied by words of caution.

A medical certification for the Beagle parents is necessary because you do not want them to pass on genetic defects which would make life difficult for the puppies. You must also ask yourself if you are certain that you will either be able to look after all the puppies, or that you will be able to find good homes for all of them. Are you also going to be able to support and care for your pets, all the way from breeding, pregnancy, the birth, and the weaning of the

Chapter Eight: Breeding Your Beagle

puppies? It's not a bad idea to ask yourself about the future of those puppies long after they have been weaned and separated from their mother. Will they be able to find a good life, in good homes?

If the above questions raises any doubts in you as to the advisability of breeding your Beagle, then do the responsible thing and have them spayed or neutered. If, on the other hand, you are still entertaining the thought of breeding your Beagle, then it is always a good idea to know everything you can about what is involved. This chapter contains some information on breeding practices which you can use as a starting point, and will hopefully encourage you to learn more.

Basic Dog Breeding Information

There are a ton of things you should have done before the actual breeding process. A careful selection of the dame and the stud, for instance, which would include some background knowledge of their temperaments, their genes, and their overall health. Make sure they have been medically certified as completely healthy by a professional.

The next thing to do is to give yourself some good background information on the canine breeding process.

Chapter Eight: Breeding Your Beagle

Make sure you have the space to devote to housing both stud and dam for at least two weeks, and that you can afford their care and the care of the puppies for the weeks after the little puppies are born well up until they are fully weaned. Aside from food, the costs would include possible medical needs and vaccinations. Needless to say, you should also have free time to be there for your pets.

The female Beagle's average age of first heat is at 6 months. This means that she is already capable of reproduction. But if you think that it is just too young, then perhaps you had better wait a season or two. Most experts do not recommend breeding immediately once she has her first heat cycle. In fact, the AKC recommends waiting until the dam is at least 8 months old. Some more conservative breeders even prefer waiting until she is at least 2 years of age. Pregnancy can be a cause of great stress for a young Beagle, so it is best to wait until she has become more mature. And not too late, either. Many veterinarians will recommend a retirement age from breeding from anywhere around 7 years of age, sometimes earlier, to avoid further compromising your Beagle's health.

And try not to breed consecutively. Some will breed every other heat cycle, while others will breed two heat cycles in a row before allowing a rest period. Consult with your veterinarian - the dam's health should always be a priority.

Chapter Eight: Breeding Your Beagle

Signs of estrus or sexual fertility (the time of heat) can be recognized by a swelling of the vulva and some bloody discarge. There should be some socialization between the dam and the stud at this time, to allow them to get comfortable with each other, hence the need for proper accommodations.

After about nine days, the female may be ready to accept the male. This is the time of greatest fertility, and will last for approximately another nine days. Most recommend breeding from the 10th to the 14th day as the peak fertile period. Once breeding is successful, mating every other day may be advisable to be sure of pregnancy, up until the female ceases to accept the male, or for two or three more matings.

The process can take an average of 45 minutes all together. At first, the male mounts the female from the rear, accompanied by rapid pelvic thrusts. Once finished, they will not separate for another 10 to 30 minutes, during which they will be positioned rear to rear. Don't try to separate them during this time because it could cause injury to either or both of them. They will part naturally once they are done.

The gestation period for most dogs lasts for an average of 63 days. You can confirm pregnancy with a veterinarian after 28 to 30 days because some females will only be showing signs of false pregnancy. Once you are

Chapter Eight: Breeding Your Beagle

certain that breeding was successful, you can prepare yourself for the pregnancy and the whelping. Take good care of your pregnant Beagle at this time, being especially careful with her diet and exercise. It is advisable that you discuss best practices with your veterinarian on their feeding and exercise schedules for the period of pregnancy.

Signs of impending labor are a change of appetite in the pregnant dam, and displays of some nesting behavior. You should already have prepared a good and roomy box some time before, to which she must have already become accustomed. Once her temperature drops to 99 degrees or lower, labor will not be far behind. You will notice that she begins panting before the contractions. The birth of each puppy will usually be preceded by panting and signs of straining or contractions.

Each puppy will come with its own placenta. The mother will usually chew or tear at the umbilical cord to free the puppy, and then begin licking the newborn to stimulate its breathing. If she neglects to do this, especially if it is her first time, you may assist her using a rough towel to clean the puppy's face and nose until it starts breathing, and using dental floss to sever the umbilical cord. Eventually, the mother herself may take over once she knows what is expected of her. Have some iodine on hand for the cut ends of the cord to prevent infection.

Chapter Eight: Breeding Your Beagle

Count the placenta. There should be one for each puppy. If the numbers don't match, it may mean that one or more were left inside the mother, which could become problematic. Call your veterinarian of this happens, or if there is any trouble with the mother or any of the puppies during whelping.

A full litter of the Beagle can number anywhere from 2 to 14 puppies. Wait it out until the dam is finished, occasionally having the newborns nurse from the mother in between the arrival of the puppies. This gives them the mother's first milk, otherwise known as the colostrum, which will provide the newborns much-needed immunity from their mother. And of course, don't forget to encourage the mother in a positive way, providing her moral support, and keeping her well-hydrated during this time.

Breeding Tips and Raising Puppies

Keep the puppies warm and safe. They will have their eyes and ears closed, which means they are completely helpless. Make sure sure they are nursing regularly. Keep the mother well-fed while she is lactating. Consult with your veterinarian about what best to feed her during this time, and how much. Ideally, however, it should be the

Chapter Eight: Breeding Your Beagle

same as during the final weeks of her pregnancy, which is some twenty to fifty percent more than her usual intake.

If the mother seems unable to feed the puppies for whatever reason - especially if it is a big litter, you can help by supplement-feeding them. Again, consult with your veterinarian on how best this should be done.

Keep the litter box clean, changing the lining often, especially once the puppies have begun urinating and defecating. They should grow fairly fast if things go well. By 2-4 weeks of age, their eyes and ears should begin to open. Socialization should already begin by this time - with simple things such as getting them accustomed to your presence. At around six weeks, they should be ready to transition to more solid food. Again, consult with your veterinarian, though a general recommendation is moistened puppy food, ideally using the same brand that you will be feeding them when they begin to mature, soaked in water or broth. Go slow, be patient, and if you are not sure, don't hesitate to ask a professional.

Tricolored Beagles are usually born black and white. The white areas will set at around 8 weeks, while some of the black areas may eventually fade to brown. There are some who will even lose their black markings completely. Bi-colored Beagles are generally born white. The puppies are fully weaned at about 8 weeks, though it is best to have

Chapter Eight: Breeding Your Beagle

them get a full examination by a veterinarian before separating them from their mother.

Arrangements for new homes should already have been made for the puppies when the dam first became pregnant. Your responsibility as a breeder extends to making sure that your puppies will be going to good homes, and to make sure that the new owners are as fully equipped as they can be to be good Beagle owners. Encourage them to register and get a license for their new puppies, and to learn as much as they can about the Beagle breed.

Chapter Nine: Showing Your Beagle

The road towards having a Beagle show dog is one that starts early, from selecting the right breed, giving him (and yourself) the proper training, and keeping him in optimal health.

How do you know if your Beagle has the potential to become a show dog champion? It may be difficult to tell when they are still puppies, and sometimes the only thing you can do is hope and pray that they will grow to perfect or near-perfect proportions, with the intelligence and the temperament to back it up. What you can do is be informed about Breed Conformation Standards and the AKC rules and regulations. Below is a general list of the AKC Official Breed Standard for Beagles.

Beagle Breed Standard

Varieties: Two - 13-inch (not exceeding 13 inches in height), and 15-inch (13-15 inches in height)

General Appearance: A miniature Foxhound, solid for his size, a hound that can last in a chase

Temperament: Cheerful at work, with points deducted for cringing, skulking or lying down

Head: Skull is fairly long, slightly domed

Ears: Set moderately low, long and reaching nearly to the end of the nose, with a fine texture, fairly broad, rounded tip, the forward edge slightly turning in at the cheek

Eyes: Brown or hazel color, set well apart, soft and houndlike expresson - gentle and pleading

Muzzle: Medium length, square cut, level jaws, nostrils large and open

Chapter Nine: Showing Your Beagle

Neck: Rising strong and free from the shoulders, throat clean and free from folds of skin

Shoulders and Chest: Clean, sloping shoulders, muscular; deep and broad chest

Legs and Feet: Straight, proportional bone structure; close, round and firm feet, ,with full and hard pads; hips and thighs strong and well-muscled

Tail: Set moderately high, carried gaily, with a slight curve, not curled over the back

Coat and Color: Any true Hound color; coat is hard, close, hound coat of medium length

Preparing Your Beagle for Show

You should be familiar with the Dog Show regulations and breed standards of the Kennel Club of your area long before you decide to compete. The assumption is that you have trained and groomed your dog months, sometimes even years, before entering.

You might also want to "scout out" the territory beforehand: visit a show and observe what's involved and what the judges seem to favor. Network. But more importantly, perhaps, bring along your Beagle to get him

Chapter Nine: Showing Your Beagle

acclimated to the sights and sounds and activities surrounding dog show events.

You should also probably learn beforehand what would be required of you during the show. How do you effectively present or show your Beagle? Ask questions and learn about what are expected and what things you should avoid doing. Make sure you have your papers in order, registered your pet in the proper category, and paid the required fees. And it goes without saying that your Beagle's health, grooming, physical condition and training should be proceeding along at a good pace. Bathing and grooming is advisable the day before the show itself.

On the fateful day, make sure you are fully prepared, your dog is fully awake and well-rested, and make sure you have packed all the essentials to bring along with you:

- Registration papers
- Water and a water bowl
- grooming kit
- show collar and leash
- trash bags
- any medication your dog may need
- toys to keep your dog amused and occupied
- snacks and treats
- paper towels

Chapter Nine: Showing Your Beagle

The most important thing, of course, is your pet. Make sure your Beagle is relaxed, well-rested, and ready for the show!

Chapter Nine: Showing Your Beagle

Chapter Ten: Keeping Your Beagle Healthy

Having been specifically bred for hunting and tracking, Beagles are generally healthy, energetic, and with the impressive stamina that goes with the job of pursuing game in the field. But there will always be the possibility of your pet developing one illness or another. This chapter contains information regarding certain ailments or health problems that seem to be common among Beagles in general. Many of them are treatable, so you should consult with your Vet at the earliest opportunity should your Beagle develop any of the symptoms listed below.

Chapter 10: Keeping Your Beagle Healthy

Common Health Problems Affecting Beagles

Epilepsy

Epilepsy is a brain dysfunction consisting of a series of confused or misfired brain signals and impulses, which can then manifest as seizures, fits, or convulsions.

While it is not accurate to say that Beagles have a genetic predisposition to epilepsy, it does seem that they are at least prone to this condition. The difficulty is that the symptoms and manifestations are so varied that even specialists are hard put to identifying specific causes or triggers.

Epileptic seizures can last from a few seconds to several minutes, and can range from mild to severe. Some of the milder symptoms can, therefore, easily be missed. It can manifest as simply staring, unresponsively, into space, odd and confused movements, or it can show itself when your pet suddenly collapses, rigidly, onto the ground. The causes can also range from a number of possibilities - from a head injury, a brain tumor, or an ear infection. When your Beagle suffers from an epileptic episode, it is advisable to bring him to a vet immediately afterwards so that it is easier for them to try to pinpoint the cause.

Chapter 10: Keeping Your Beagle Healthy

This is also a potentially chronic condition, which means that it can last for several years, so an accurate diagnosis is always desirable because it will help you in managing your pet's lifestyle to avoid or treat identified triggers. But be prepared for the frustration of not knowing precisely why your Beagle is suffering from epilepsy. Much is still not known about canine epilepsy, though there are ways of managing the condition, mainly through anticonvulsant medication.

Once diagnosed, you can also make sure that your Beagle will not be in any danger should he suffer from an epileptic attack even when nobody is around at the time. Keep him confined in a safe room or yard where there are no potential sources of danger to your pet - such as open sources of water or fire and sharp and piercing objects.

There are distinct signs you can watch out for that would alert you to the onset of an epileptic seizure. Such seizures usually occur in three stages, and Beagles would display unusual or abnormal behavior in the first stage, such as nervousness, disorientation, or anxiety. Once you recognize your pet acting differently, you can better prepare yourself for the second stage, or the seizure itself.

During the epileptic episode, your pet may lose consciousness, his limbs may grow rigid, and he can suddenly lose control of his bowels and release urine or feces. First of all, be calm. Provide a sense of safety to your

Chapter 10: Keeping Your Beagle Healthy

pet by reassuring him with your presence, talking to him in a gentle voice, and keeping him warm in a blanket until the episode passes.

In the third phase, your Beagle may still show some signs of disorientation, restlessness and even depression. In some instances, this can last for a few days, especially if the seizure was severe.

Take heart if your Beagle has become diagnosed with epilepsy. It is usually not life-threatening. And if you manage to adjust yourself to these episodes, seek professional advice and treatment, your Beagle can still live a long and healthy life

Hypothyroidism

Beagles are also recognized to be predisposed to Hypothyroidism, which is an endocrine problem consisting of low levels of thyroid hormones in the blood. The thyroid gland is reponsible for a hormone that controls metabolism, which means that the dog's metabolism is slower. Growth and development, and even immunity, are also compromised.

Manifestations of this condition are varied, and can include weight gain disproportionate to his appetite, low tolerance to temperature changes, sluggishness or lack of energy, skin conditions such as dryness of hair, hair loss, discoloration or skin infections, and may even manifest in behavior changes such as seizures or epilepsy, anxiety, aggression and lethargy.

Hypothyroidism usually happens in middle age, well past breeding age, and it is difficult to catch because many of the milder symptoms can simply be taken as signs of growing old. That is why it is important to have regular checkups with your vet so that this condition can be caught as early as possible. Once diagnosed, it can last for your pet's lifetime, but when treatment is started early, the prospects are generally good.

Treatment consists of taking supplemental thyroid hormones, and will have to continue for the rest of his life.

Chondrodystrophy or Dwarfism

Also otherwise known as osteochondrodysplasia or chondrodysplasia, this is a genetic condition which usually affect the long bones of the legs, though it can sometimes also affect the skull and the spine. These skeletal abnormalities result in a "dwarf" dog, or one who is unusually small or underdeveloped.

Being genetic, the cause is having one or both parents as carriers of the gene that causes this defect, though it can

Chapter 10: Keeping Your Beagle Healthy

also be caused by other factors such as malnutrition, hypothyroidism and other hormonal imbalances. The sad reality is that no matter how careful and cautious a breeder is, sometimes this condition can just manifest in a litter of newborn puppies. To date, there is no gene test specific to Beagles, and most professionals advise that any Beagle who has produced a dwarf puppy, or who manifest even the slightest sign or symptom of the disease, should simply not be bred.

The signs become apparent early, and one can usually identify the puppy in the litter whose growth seems to be stunted, or whose legs or skull seem out of proportion to the rest of his body, though the primary manifestation is in shortened legs.

A physical checkup with a vet would involve urinalysis, blood work, and x-rays to observe the dog's skeletal development, as well as an examination of the dog's medical history. The condition itself is not difficult to identify.

Its manifestations can range from mild to severe. For some, it only leads to some minor discomfort such as clumsiness in walking. For others, it can cause pain in the joints and and legs, less activity, and the possible development of arthritis and joint problems. It is possible, however, to manage the condition with anti-inflammatories and therapy.

For the more severe cases, however, which would involve multiple skeletal abnormalities, the dog would be completely incapable of living a normal life, and would likely be in severe pain for the rest of his life. In such instances, professionals recommend that the most humane thing to do would be euthanasia.

Hip Dysplasia

There are some of the opinion that Hip Dysplasia is pretty uncommon in Beagles, but it is not unheard of. Perhaps it is because it does not usually manifest in the breed until their older years, exacerbated by other factors such as obesity or too much exercise, though there must be a genetic tendency for the problem to develop in the first place.

In such a condition, there is an abnormality in the development of a dog's hip joint, which causes stiffness, pain, limping, or the adopting an abnormal gait such as bunny-hopping. The symptoms can range from mild to severe, and can be treated by medication for pain relief, or surgery in some instances.

Since hip dysplasia is a genetic condition, it is always a good idea to verify your pet's medical records before bringing him home. You can also reduce the incidence of the condition in the first place by keeping your Beagle from becoming obese, and by not over-exercising them. Once diagnosed, consult with your vet to determine the best treatment programs - this would usually consist of supplements, therapy and a mild exercise program.

Cherry Eye

Cherry Eye is another congenital or genetic condition which some breeds are prone to, and that would include Beagles. Basically, this involves a weakness in the connective tissues in a dog's eyelid which leads to a prolapse of the tear gland in the nictitating membrane, causing it to protrude in a visible corner of the eyeball. The appearance of the red gland in the corner of your dog's eyes is what led to the term "cherry eye."

It can happen in one or both eyes, but the condition itself is not painful, though it can lead to other complications such as bacterial or viral infections, which might compromise overall eye health.

There are currently three possible treatments for cherry eye. Most veterinarians prefer surgical treatment, which would entail either stitching the prolapsed tear gland back in place, or the creation of an artificial pocket or

Chapter 10: Keeping Your Beagle Healthy

envelope that would be able to permanently hold the gland in place.

There are other advocates of a less invasive treatment, which involves the use of eye drops and massaging gently over the closed eyelid of the dog, eventually popping the gland back in its place. Recurrence is common in such situations, though some claim that the regular massage can actually help to strengthen the connective tissues in the eyelids. Some experts, however, caution that this might actually exacerbate the condition since you are dealing with the eyes, which are very delicate.

A third option, and usually only recommended as a last resort, is the surgical removal of the protruding tear gland. If your pet's condition is caught early, then you may not have to take this option. Basically, this entails the complete removal of the tear gland, causing dry eyes and insufficient lubrication, which will then require lifelong treatment with artificial tears.

Allergies

Beagles are also prone to developing allergies. This is another genetic condition, though the possible allergens can vary. It's always a frustrating situation to try to figure out what exactly your Beagle may be allergic to, though common things to watch out for are certain foods, fleas or bugs, some kinds of pet shampoo, home products, plants, even dust! Consult with your veterinarian to verify the diagnosis, and for help in tracing the cause and in planning out the possible treatment options.

Signs to watch out for are constant itching, dry skin and hair, sneezing, constant licking and biting, and runny or itchy eyes.

The main solution to this condition is the removal of the cause of the allergies. Keep your pet from coming into further contact with the allergen. The symptoms themselves can be treated with medication.

Obesity

The incidence of canine obesity in the United States has recently grown to an alarming rate. And while many dogs from different breeds might suffer from obesity, the Beagle is one breed that is particualrly prone to being overweight.

Why is this so? The causes might not be very difficult to pinpoint. Too much eating and not enough exercise are usually the main culprits. And Beagles in particular are very fond of eating. Some call them "chow-hounds," and they literally have the capacity for endless eating. Couple that

Chapter 10: Keeping Your Beagle Healthy

with their very endearing brown eyes that always seem to convey to you a state of pitiable hunger, many owners relent and feed their Beagles, even though their pet may have just had a full meal not an hour ago.

The only real way to treat Beagle obesity is by giving them what they previously lacked: exercise and a proper diet. If your Beagle is already dangerously obese, consult first with a professional to figure out a safe and workable diet and exercise plan.

But responsible owners really shouldn't allow it to go too far. Pay attention to your pet: signs of obesity aren't difficult to spot. If you look at them from above, you should see that they have a noticeable waist, and from below, the chest should be lower than the belly. If you notice them becoming a bit heavy and bulky around the waist, increase their exercise and decrease their food intake. The key is making small changes. Never take any drastic measures in either your dog's diet or daily exercise without the approval of a veterinarian.

Obesity can cause, or exacerbate may other difficult health conditions such as joint problems, heart disease or even diabetes, so obesity is a very serious concern. If, on the other hand, your Beagle seems to be gaining weight persistently despite regular diet and exercise, and without any major changes in their food intake, or if they do not seem to have increased appetite anyway, bring him to a vet immediately. It may be that he is suffering from some other underlying condition that promotes unhealthy weight gain.

Musladin-Lueke Syndrome (MLS)

Also called the Chinese Beagle Syndrome, this is a genetic condition characterized by stiff legs, shortened toes in the front legs, the back legs, or all four, and tight skin resulting in a hard and seemingly well-muscled body and the absence of a "ruff." The head has a noticeable flat skull, with the ears set higher and slanting eyes. The tail is held straight and stiff, with some noticeable kinks. It can be diagnosed as early as 2 to 4 weeks.

This syndrome was named after Drs. Tony and Judy Musladin and Ada Lueke, who discovered it sometime in the early 1990s. Take note that the only way to be certain whether your Beagle is suffering from this condition is to have them tested There is a genetic marker test now available to screen for this condition. Don't guess or self-diagnose - there are many Beagles who may manifest one or more of the symptoms but are actually perfectly healthy. The test itself generally costs around USD50, so it is not very expensive.

Avoid breeding dogs who are suffering from, or are carriers of this syndrome. On the other hand, those who have been diagnosed will need all the support you can give them, which would include regular checkups with a vet, particularly to monitor the condition of their eyes, their legs and toes, and the condition of their muscles and limbs. It is also possible that Beagles with MLS might suffer from diminished intelligence, so a little patience in dealing with them - especially during housetraining - can go a long way in helping them.

Preventing Illness with Vaccinations

There is recent debate regarding the necessity of annual booster shots. Some are claiming they are not needed quite as often as they are usually administered.

Regardless of where you stand on the vaccinationa debate, however, there are standard vaccines that all dogs, including Beagles, will need.

Vaccines boost the body's immunity by stimulating the creation of antibodies that work against foreign organisms.

Newborns have a natural immunity which they absorb from the umbilical cord while they are still in the womb, but this does not last long, and may wear off before the puppy's immune system has fully kicked in. That is why it is important to have them take their mother's first milk, or colostrum, because it also provides them with protection, though again it is only temporary, usually lasting only for the first two days. This level of protection derived from the mother, it must be noted, only works to provide them with antibodies against those diseases for which the mother had been vaccinated against.

When both of these natural protection have worn off, then it is time for vaccines. Below is a standard vaccination schedule for Beagles:

Vaccination Schedule for Beagles **	
Age	Vaccine
5 weeks	Parvovirus
6-8 weeks	Adenovirus, Distemper, Hepatitis, Parainfluenza, Parvovirus
12 weeks	Rabies and Leptospirosis
14 weeks	Lyme Disease and Leptospirosis
16 weeks	Leptospirosis

** Keep in mind that vaccine requirements may vary from one region to another. Only your vet will be able to tell you which vaccines are most important for the region where you live.

Chapter 10: Keeping Your Beagle Healthy

For adult Beagles, no matter which side of the debate on annual booster shots you agree with, it is an absolute requirement that your Beagle receive a yearly vaccine for rabies. This is legally required, and in many states, is coterminous with the yearly renewal of your pet license.

Always do your homework and consult with a professional. The above is simply a standard vaccination schedule, and is considered variable depending on your veterinarian's recommendation, who will base his advice on the needs generated by the region you live in, and a specific examination of your Beagle's state of health.

Chapter 10: Keeping Your Beagle Healthy

Chapter 10: Keeping Your Beagle Healthy

Beagle Care Sheet

1.) Basic Beagle Information

Pedigree: Talbot Hound, North Country Beagle, Southern Hound, and the Harrier

AKC Group: Hound Group

Chapter 10: Keeping Your Beagle Healthy

Types: In the AKC, distinction is made between two sizes - the 13-inch Beagle (no taller than 13 inches at the withers), and the 15-inch Beagle (between 13 and 15 inches at the withers). No size distinction is made in the Kennel Groups in other countries.

Breed Size: small to medium size

Height: 13 to 16 inches (33 to 41 cm) high at the withers

Weight: 20 to 25 lb (9-11 kg)

Coat Length: medium length

Coat Texture: close and hard, hound coat

Color: Varied, may be tricolor or bi-color, usually of white, brown and black, with white as the predominant color, a black saddle, and tan or brown markings around the saddle. Bi-colors usually have white as the predominant color, with the secondary color as reddish, orange, liver, or blue (smoky gray).

Eyes and Nose: Dark brown or hazel eyes, black or gumdrop nose

Ears: Floppy or dropped ears, set slightly above the eyes and hanging close to the head

Tail: Set fairly high, short and slightly curved, with a white tip. It is held upright or carried in a jaunty fashion, and does not curve over the back.

Chapter 10: Keeping Your Beagle Healthy

Temperament: Friendly, has an even temper and gentle disposition; amiable. A bit excitable, easily distracted or bored.

Strangers: Beagles will bark or howl at anything or anyone unfamiliar, but they can be easily won over. They make good watchdogs but poor guard dogs.

Other Dogs: Beagles generally get along well with other dogs.

Other Pets: Generally friendly with other pets, and are actually quite gentle with cats.

Training: Difficult to train. Beagles are intelligent, but having been bred to be scenthounds, they are single-minded and focused when they pick up a scent. They are easily distracted by the smells around them. Obedience is not very high.

Exercise Needs: Regular moderate exercise such as daily walks, with occasional intense bursts of exercise such as running at least once a week.

Health Conditions: epilepsy, hypothyroidism, chondrodystrophy or dwarfism, hip dysplasia, cherry eye, allergies, obesity, Musladin-Lueke Syndrome (MLS)

Lifespan: average 12-15 years

Chapter 10: Keeping Your Beagle Healthy

2.) Habitat Requirements

Recommended Accessories: dog bed, food/water dishes, toys, collar, leash, harness, grooming supplies

Collar and Harness: sized by weight

Grooming Supplies: bristle brush, hound glove with raised rubber nodes, or rubber curry

Grooming Frequency: Brush once or twice a week; bathing can be done monthly or when he starts to get dirty or smelly.

Energy Level: high energy level; lack of exercise can lead to destructive behavior

Exercise Requirements: Balance long walks with occasional short walks and playtime.

Food/Water: stainless steel or ceramic bowls, clean daily

Toys: start with an assortment, see what the dog likes; include some mentally stimulating toys

3.) Nutritional Needs

Nutritional Needs: water, protein, carbohydrate, fats, vitamins, minerals

RER: 30(body weight in kilograms) + 70

Chapter 10: Keeping Your Beagle Healthy

Calorie Needs: varies by age, weight, and activity level; RER modified with activity level

Amount to Feed (puppy): Scheduled feeding 3x a day should commence at around 3-6 months, working your way down to 2 meals after 6 months, and 1 full meal after 1 year. This will make room for the snacks and treats needed during training.

Amount to Feed (adult): consult recommendations on the package; calculated by weight. Feed once a day, and monitor the snacks or treats intake.

Important Ingredients: fresh animal protein (chicken, beef, lamb, turkey, eggs), digestible carbohydrates (rice, oats, barley), animal fats

Important Minerals: calcium, phosphorus, potassium, magnesium, iron, copper and manganese

Important Vitamins: Vitamin A, Vitamin A, Vitamin B-12, Vitamin D, Vitamin C

Look For: AAFCO statement of nutritional adequacy; protein at top of ingredients list; no artificial flavors, dyes, preservatives

Chapter 10: Keeping Your Beagle Healthy

4.) Breeding Information

Age of First Heat: Around 6 months old, sometimes earlier or later by a few months

Heat (Estrus) Cycle: 14 to 21 days

Frequency: twice a year, every 5 to 7 months

Greatest Fertility: 11 to 15 days into the cycle

Gestation Period: 59 to 63 days

Pregnancy Detection: possible after 21 days, best to wait 28-30 days before exam

Feeding Pregnant Dogs: maintain normal diet until week 4 or 5 then slightly increase rations by 20 to 50 percent for the last five weeks

Signs of Labor: body temperature drops below normal 100° to 102°F (37.7° to 38.8°C), may be as low as 98°F (36.6°C); dog begins nesting in a dark, quiet place

Contractions: period of 10 minutes in waves of 3 to 5 followed by a period of rest

Whelping: may last for about two to four hours or more, depending on the litter size

Puppies: born with eyes and ears closed; eyes open at 3 weeks, teeth develop at 10 weeks

Chapter 10: Keeping Your Beagle Healthy

Litter Size: average 2 to 14 puppies

Size at Birth: about 5-10 oz.

Weaning: supplement with controlled portions of moistened puppy food at around 4 weeks, or when the mother starts losing interest in feeding the puppies. Fully weaned at 7-8 weeks

Socialization: start as early as possible to prevent puppies from being nervous as an adult, preferably before 14-16 weeks of age

Chapter 10: Keeping Your Beagle Healthy

Index

A

AFCO	105
Adopting from a Rescue	5, 30
age	6, 105
Age of First Heat	106
AKC	2, 4
AKC Group	
Hound Group	13, 101
Alcohol	53
Allergies	7, 93, 94, 130
Crate	4
Amount to Feed	105
appearance	3, 4, 5
Apple seeds	53
Australia Rescues	6, 31
Avocado	53
award	2

B

Babbler	2
Balance	2
Basic Beagle information	8, 101
Basic Dog Breeding Information	7, 6, 72, 106
Bay	2
Beagle Breed History	5, 15
Beagle Breed Standard	7, 80
Beagle Care Sheet	8, 101
Beagle-Proofing Your Home	6, 34, 35
Beagle Rescues	30, 31
Beagle Standard	18
Beagle Ownership	21
behavior	3, 4

Best in Show	2
Bicolor	2
bitch	2, 4
bowls	104
breed	3, 5, 6
breeder	6, 32
breeding	73
Breed Size	13, 102
Breed Standard	3, 81
breeding	5, 7, 71, 76

C

cage	4
Calorie Needs	105
Can be loud pets to keep	28
canine eye wipes	65
caring for	6, 39, 79
Crossbreed	4
carbohydrates	6, 47, 105
care	3
castrate	3, 6
Character	3
Cherry Eye	7, 92, 133
Cherry pits	53
Chocolate	53
Chondrodystrophy or Dwarfism	7, 89
Citrus	53
Cleaning Your Beagle's Ears	7, 66
coat and color	3, 4, 5, 6, 7, 13, 81, 102
Coconut	53
Coffee	53
Collar and Harness	104
Conformation	4
Cons for the Beagles	5, 28
Contractions during Pregnancy	106
cost	5, 25, 26, 27, 49
Crate Training	6, 58
Cry	4

D

dam	4, 6
Dangerous Foods	6, 52
diet	51, 106
dog food	6, 48, 77
dog show regulations	81
Dominance	4
double coat	3
Drop Ear	4
Dwarfism	90

E

ears	4, 5, 14, 67, 80, 102, 106
eating	7
Energy Level	104
Epilepsy	7, 86, 88, 130, 134
Even bite	4
Exercise Needs	6, 15, 41, 103, 104
eye	2, 3, 14, 80, 102, 106

F

Facts about Beagles	5, 10
fats	6, 47, 104, 105
feeding	6, 51
Feeding Pregnant Dogs	106
female	2, 4, 6, 7
Fetch	5
field trials	13
food	7, 104
friendliness	10, 24

G

Gait	5

Games	5, 60, 61
Garlic	53
gene	3
genealogy	5, 6
General Appearance	80
Gestation Period	5, 106
Grapes/raisins	53
Greatest Fertility	106
grooming	5, 7, 63, 64, 65, 66, 68, 69, 82, 104

H

Habitat	6, 8, 40, 104
hair	2, 3, 5, 7
harness	104
Head	80
health	4, 7, 15, 85, 103
health problems	7, 86
Heat	5, 106
Heel	5
Height	13, 102
herding	104
Hip Dysplasia	5, 7, 5, 91, 134, 135
Hops	53
Hound	5
Hound-colors	5
Housetraining	28
Hypothyroidism	7, 15, 88, 89, 103, 131, 136, 138

I

Initial Costs	5, 25
Intelligence	28
Interbreeding	5

K

kennel	4, 6

L

Lead - Leash	6, 104
legs	5, 81
Leptospirosis	98, 107
license	5, 22
Lifespan	15, 103
litter	6, 7, 107
Lyme Disease	98

M

Macadamia nuts	53
male	6, 7
Mate	6
milk	7, 53
minerals	104
Mold	53
Mongrel	6
Mushrooms	53
Musladin-Lueke Syndrome (MLS)	8, 15, 96, 103
Mustard seeds	53
Muzzle	80

N

Neck	81
Neuter	6
noisy	28, 40
Nutritional Needs	6, 8, 45, 46, 47, 48, 104, 105

O

obesity	7, 15, 94, 95, 103, 133
Onions/leeks	53
Other Dogs	5, 14, 24, 25, 28, 103
Other Grooming Tasks	7, 66

Other initial costs to factor in include:	25
outer coat	7
Overall health	28

P

Pack	6, 23, 28, 40
Pads	6
paper towels	82
parent	4, 7
Parvovirus	98
Peach pits	53
Pedigree	6, 13, 101
Point	6
Poisonous or toxic plants	36
Positive Reinforcement and Rewards	6, 38, 61
Potato leaves/stems	53
Pregnancy Detection	106
Preparing Your Beagle for Show	7, 81
Pros for Beagles	5, 28
protein	6, 46, 104, 105
puppies	6, 7, 8, 33, 105, 106
purchasing	5, 29
purebred	2, 6

R

Rabies and Leptospirosis	98
Raw meat and eggs	53
Recommended Accessories	7, 64, 104
record	6
Registration papers	82
registry	2
RER	50, 104
Retrieve	7
Rhubarb leaves	53

S

Saddle	7
Salty snacks	53
safety	35, 36
scenthound	2, 9, 10, 17
Shoulders and Chest	81
show	2, 7, 79, 82, 83
Signs of Labor	106
sire	4, 6, 7
Size at Birth	107
skin	4, 6
skull	2
snacks and treats	45, 82, 105
Socialization	6, 25, 56, 107
spay	6, 7
Strangers	14, 103
Stud	7
Summary of Beagle Facts	5, 13
supervision	28, 35
supplies	104
surgery	7

T

tail	4, 5, 14, 81, 102
Tea	53
teeth	3, 106
Temperament	14, 28, 80, 103
Tomato leaves/stems	53
toys	82, 104
Training	6, 15, 28, 55, 56, 61, 103
Tricolor	7
Trimming Your Beagle's Nails	7, 68
Types	5, 7, 13, 18, 80, 102

U

undercoat	3, 7, 104
United Kingdom Rescues	5, 31, 32
United States Rescues	5, 30

V

Vaccinations	8, 97, 98, 99, 106
Varieties	80
vitamins	6, 47, 104

W

Walnuts	53
water	82, 104
Weaning	7, 107
weight	13, 102, 104, 105
Whelping	7, 106
white	3, 6

X

Xylitol	53

Y

yard	40
Yeast dough	53

Photo Credits

Cover Page Photo By Taz80 / SEDIRI Eddy via Wikimedia Commons.
<https://commons.wikimedia.org/wiki/File:Beagle_Faraon.JPG>

Page 1 Photo By Berndf via Wikimedia Commons.
<https://commons.wikimedia.org/wiki/File:Beagle_tan-white.jpg>

Page 9 Photo By Jimmy van Hoorn <http://flickr.com/photos/22215758@N08/2385729492> as Uploaded to Wikimedia Commons by Ltshears <https://commons.wikimedia.org/wiki/File:Beagle_001.jpg>

Page 21 Photo By Lilly M via Wikimedia Commons <https://commons.wikimedia.org/wiki/File:Baegle_dwa.jpg>

Page 29 Photo By Juanelverdolaga via Wikimedia Commons <https://commons.wikimedia.org/wiki/File:Beagle_puppy_sitting_on_grass.jpg>

Page 39 Photo by Vmars-commonswiki via Wikimedia Commons <https://commons.wikimedia.org/wiki/File:Beagle2.JPG>

Page 45 Photo By Doniu013 via Wikimedia Commons <https://commons.wikimedia.org/wiki/File:Beagle55.JPG>

Page 55 Photo by Karen Arnold via Wikimedia Commons <https://commons.wikimedia.org/wiki/File:Beagle-dog.jpg>

Page 63 Photo by Claude Valroff via Wikimedia Commons <https://commons.wikimedia.org/wiki/File:Beagle_Upsy.jpg>

Page 71 Photo by D. Mighton via Wikimedia Commons <https://commons.wikimedia.org/wiki/File:Beagles_Puppies.png>

Page 79 Photo by en:sannse via Wikimedia Commons <https://commons.wikimedia.org/wiki/File:Beagle_Upsy.jpg>

Page 85 Photo by Jeff Pearce <https://www.flickr.com/photos/11916736@N00/215155210/>

Page 101 Photo by Howcheng <https://www.flickr.com/photos/malingering/110378744/>

References

"A Diet for Beagles." Team Petcarerx. <https://www.petcarerx.com/article/a-diet-for-beagles/468>

"American Kennel Club." akc.org. <http://www.akc.org/about/glossary/>

"Avoid Having a Fat Beagle." National Beagle Club. <http://clubs.akc.org/NBC/fat_beagle.html>

"Beagle." dogtime.com <http://dogtime.com/dog-breeds/beagle>

"Beagle." Wikipedia.org. <https://en.m.wikipedia.org/wiki/Beagle>

"Beagle Allergies." Sharon Becker. <http://beaglehappy.com/beagle-allergies.html>

"Beagles and Dwarfism." terrificpets.com. <http://www.terrificpets.com/articles/102146065.asp>

"Beagles & Epilepsy." beaglerescueleague.org. <http://www.beaglerescueleague.org/beagle-info/common-beagle-health-concerns/common-beagle-health-concerns-part-ii>

"Beagle Command Training." beaglepro.com. <http://www.beaglepro.com/beagle-command-training>

"Beagle Information and Pictures." dogbreedinfo.com. <http://www.dogbreedinfo.com/beagle.htm>

"Beagle Exercise." beaglepro.com.
<http://www.beaglepro.com/beagle-exercise>

"Beagle Grooming." beaglepro.com.
<http://www.beaglepro.com/beagle-grooming>

"Beagle Grooming Basics." DogChannel.com.
<http://www.dogchannel.com/dog-information/dog-groomer-salzberg/beagle-grooming-basics.aspx>

"Beagle Health." Sam Goldberg.
<http://www.beaglewelfare.org.uk/beagle_health.html>

"Beagle Proofing Your Home." Kris Kraeuter.
<http://www.safehounds.com/documents/Beagle_Proof.html>

"Beagle Puppy Training & Breed Information." Dog Training Central. <http://www.dog-obedience-training-review.com/beagle-puppy-training.html#Beagle>

"Beagle Seizures." beaglepro.com.
<http://www.beaglepro.com/beagle-seizures>

"Beagle Vaccinations." beaglepro.com.
<http://www.beaglepro.com/beagle-vaccinations>

"Beagle: Hypothyroidism." UFAW.
<http://www.ufaw.org.uk/dogs/beagle-hypothyroidism>

"Beagle - Beagle Dwarfism, and Other Maladies." aboutbeagles.aussieblogs.com.

<http://aboutbeagles.aussieblogs.com.au/2013/03/31/beagles-beagle-dwarfism-and-other-maladies/>

"Beagles - Vaccinations Pros and Cons." aboutbeagles.aussieblogs.com. <http://aboutbeagles.aussieblogs.com.au/2013/03/31/beagles-vaccination-pros-and-cons/>

"Beagling." Wikipedia. <https://en.wikipedia.org/wiki/Beagling>

"Bone Deformity and Dwarfism in Dogs." petmd.com. <http://www.petmd.com/dog/conditions/Musculoskeletal/c_dg_osteochondrodysplasia#>

"Breeding a Beagle." beaglepro.com. <http://www.beaglepro.com/beagle-breeding>

"Canine Terms, Dog Words, Dog Terms." dogbreedinfo.com. <http://www.dogbreedinfo.com/terms.htm>

"Caring for Beagles." Nicole Pajer. <https://www.cesarsway.com/about-dogs/breeds/caring-for-beagles>

"Causes and Prevention of Dwarfism in Dogs." petwave.com. <http://www.petwave.com/Dogs/Health/Dwarfism/Causes.aspx>

"Cherry Eye in Dogs." pets4homes.co.uk. <http://www.pets4homes.co.uk/pet-advice/cherry-eye-in-dogs.html>

"Cherry Eye in Dogs: Tips on Prevention and Treatment." Melvin Peña. <http://www.dogster.com/lifestyle/cherry-eye-in-dogs-dog-health-facts-tips-prevention-treatment>

"Chinese Beagle Syndrome." National Beagle Club. <http://clubs.akc.org/NBC/mls.html>

"Cost of Owning a Dog: Averages & Most Expensive Breeds." John S. Kiernan. <https://wallethub.com/edu/cost-of-owning-a-dog/15563/>

"Diagnosing Dwarfism in Dogs." petwave.com. <http://www.petwave.com/Dogs/Health/Dwarfism/Diagnosis.aspx>

"Dog Breeds Prone to Obesity." Ann Staub. <http://www.mypawsitivelypets.com/2014/02/dog-breeds-prone-to-obesity.html>

"Dwarfism in Beagles." beaglesunlimited.com. <http://www.beaglesunlimited.com/health/dwarfism-beagles>

"Dwarfism in Beagles." John Buckley. <http://www.beagleinformation.com/beagle-health/dwarfism-in-beagles/>

"Dwarfism in Dogs." petwave.com <www.petwave.com/Dogs/Health/Dwarfism.aspx>

"Epilepsy." Ada Lueke. <http://www.aladarbeagles.com/epilepsy.html>

"Epilepsy and Elipeptic Seizures." beaglesunlimited.com. <http://www.beaglesunlimited.com/health/epilepsy-and-epileptic-seizures>

"Epilepsy in Beagles." beaglehealth.info. <http://www.beaglehealth.info/general%20pages/epilepsy.html>

"Excerpts from Comments from Alliance for Animals Post Card." aladarbeagles.com. <http://www.aladarbeagles.com/spca.html>

"Getting Started in Beagling." AKC. <http://www.akc.org/events/field-trials/beagles/getting-started/>

"Grooming Tips for Beagles." Alex Katz. <http://www.newsmax.com/FastFeatures/gun-dog-breeders-beagle-grooming/2016/01/21/id/710377/>

"Hip Dysplasia in Beagles." Dog's Health.com. <https://dogshealth.com/blog/hip-dysplasia-in-beagles/>

"Hip Dysplasia in Beagles." Ruth Darlene Stewart. <http://www.aladarbeagles.com/hd2.html>

"Hip Dysplasia in Dogs." webmd.com. <http://pets.webmd.com/dogs/canine-hip-dysplasia>

"House Training." Triangle Beagle Rescue of North Carolina. <http://tribeagles.org/house-training/>

"How Do You Pick a Puppy?" John Rogers Jr. <http://www.beaglesunlimited.com/other/how-do-you-pick-puppy>

"How Much to Feed a Dog to Meet his Energy Needs." Drs. Foster & Smith. <http://www.peteducation.com/article.cfm?c=2+1659&aid=2612>

"How to Beagle Proof Your House." welovebeagles.com. <http://www.welovebeagles.com/how-to-beagle-proof-your-house/>

"How to Care for a Beagle with Chinese Beagle Syndrome." Rhomylly Forbes. <http://www.ehow.com/how_7364256_care-beagle-chinese-beagle-syndrome.html>

"How to Exercise your Beagle." welovebeagles.com. <http://www.welovebeagles.com/how-to-exercise-your-beagle/>

"How to Groom a Beagle." Susan McCullough. <http://www.dummies.com/how-to/content/how-to-groom-a-beagle.html>

"How to Help Food-Obsessed Beagles Lose Weight." Susan Paretts. <http://pets.thenest.com/foodobsessed-beagles-lose-weight-6253.html>

"How Much Exercise Do Dogs Need Each Day?" Linda Cole. <http://www.canidae.com/blog/2014/06/how-much-exercise-do-dogs-need-each-day/>

"Hypothyroidism in Beagle Dogs." beaglesunlimited.com. <http://www.beaglesunlimited.com/health/hypothyroidism-beagle-dogs>

"Hypothyroidism in Beagles." beagleinformation.com. <http://www.beagleinformation.com/beagle-health/hypothyroidism-beagles/>

"Hypothyroidism in Dogs." pets.webmd. <http://pets.webmd.com/dogs/hypothyroidism-in-dogs>

"Is the Beagle the Right Breed for You?" Susan McCullough. <http://www.dummies.com/how-to/content/is-the-beagle-the-right-breed-for-you.html>

"Is Your Beagle Overweight?" beaglestothe rescue.org. <http://www.beaglestotherescue.org/canine-obesity>

"Man's best Spend! The Shocking Cost of Owning a Dog Over its Lifetime." Marianne Power. <http://www.dailymail.co.uk/femail/article-1292819/Mans-best-spend-The-shocking-cost-owning-dog-lifetime.html>

"New to Dog Showing?" The Kennel Club. <http://www.thekennelclub.org.uk/activities/dog-showing/new-to-dog-showing/>

"Official Standard for the Beagle." American Kennel Club. <http://images.akc.org/pdf/breeds/standards/Beagle.pdf?_ga=1.108250560.312113990.1460307006>

"Preparing for a Dog Show." yourdog.co.uk. <http://www.yourdog.co.uk/Dog-Activities/preparing-for-a-dog-show.html>

"Pros and Cons of Owning Beagles." pethelpful.com. <https://pethelpful.com/dogs/Pros-and-Cons-of-Owning-Beagles>

"Puppy Proofing the House and Yard." marcnadine.com. <http://www.marcnadine.com/Puppy_tips/Entries/2010/10/4_Afternoon_at_the_park.html>

"Responsible Breeding." AKC. <http://www.akc.org/dog-breeders/responsible-breeding/>

"Symptoms of Dwarfism in Dogs." petwave.com. <http://www.petwave.com/Dogs/Health/Dwarfism/Symptoms.aspx>

"The 10 Dog Breeds with the Best Sense of Smell." Kim Campbell Thornton. <http://dogtime.com/dog-health/general/18724-10-dog-breeds-with-the-best-sense-of-smell>

"The Annual Cost of Pet Ownership: Can You Afford a Furry Friend?" David Weliver. <http://www.moneyunder30.com/the-true-cost-of-pet-ownership>

"Training Beagles." yourpurebredpuppy.com. <http://www.yourpurebredpuppy.com/training/beagles.html>

"Treatment and Prognosis for Dwarfism in Dogs." petwave.com. <http://www.petwave.com/Dogs/Health/Dwarfism/Treatment.aspx>

"Vaccinations." brankosbeagles. <http://www.brankosbeagles.com/advice-vaccinations.html>

"Want to Do Well at the Dog Show? Prepare All You Can Ahead of Time." AKC. <http://www.akc.org/learn/family-dog/prepare-ahead-of-time/>

"Your Dog Has Hypothyroidism - or Does She?" healthypets.mercola.com. <healthypets.mercola.com/sites/healthypets/archive/2010/09/30/hypothyroidism-symptoms-and-prevention-in-pet-dogs.aspx

Feeding Baby
Cynthia Cherry
978-1941070000

Axolotl
Lolly Brown
978-0989658430

Dysautonomia, POTS Syndrome
Frederick Earlstein
978-0989658485

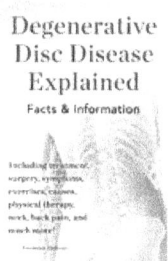

Degenerative Disc Disease Explained
Frederick Earlstein
978-0989658485

Sinusitis, Hay Fever,
Allergic Rhinitis Explained
Frederick Earlstein
978-1941070024

Wicca
Riley Star
978-1941070130

Zombie Apocalypse
Rex Cutty
978-1941070154

Capybara
Lolly Brown
978-1941070062

Eels As Pets
Lolly Brown
978-1941070167

Scabies and Lice Explained
Frederick Earlstein
978-1941070017

Saltwater Fish As Pets
Lolly Brown
978-0989658461

Torticollis Explained
Frederick Earlstein
978-1941070055

Kennel Cough
Lolly Brown
978-0989658409

Physiotherapist, Physical Therapist
Christopher Wright
978-0989658492

Rats, Mice, and Dormice As Pets
Lolly Brown
978-1941070079

Wallaby and Wallaroo Care
Lolly Brown
978-1941070031

Bodybuilding Supplements
Explained
Jon Shelton
978-1941070239

Demonology
Riley Star
978-19401070314

Pigeon Racing
Lolly Brown
978-1941070307

Dwarf Hamster
Lolly Brown
978-1941070390

Cryptozoology
Rex Cutty
978-1941070406

Eye Strain
Frederick Earlstein
978-1941070369

Inez The Miniature Elephant
Asher Ray
978-1941070353

Vampire Apocalypse
Rex Cutty
978-1941070321

www.ingramcontent.com/pod-product-compliance
Lightning Source LLC
Chambersburg PA
CBHW061442040426
42450CB00007B/1169